For you Dad,

Happy Birthday

May you have many more.

Love you always

Mark.

D0453157

Penguin Books
The Hardy Guides Volume 2

Hermann Lea was born in 1869 at Thorpe-Le-Soken, Essex, and died three days before his eighty-third birthday, one of the few surviving personal friends of Thomas Hardy. As a young man, Lea became a pupil of Mr Wood Home at Athelhampton Hall to learn farming, but he was more devoted to dogs, horse-riding and tennis. His love of animals prompted him to become a vegetarian and he was known, on occasions, to attack anyone he saw ill-treating an animal.

Keenly interested in natural history, many of the observations he made provided valuable records in that field. His skills lay too in building, bee-keeping, gardening and poultry farming. He was also greatly interested in witchcraft and he wrote several articles on the subject. Lea did a great deal of his writing, including articles for *The Animals' Friend*, in a small wooden house he built in the garden of his house at Higher Bockhampton, which had been the birthplace and home of Hardy.

It was photography, however, that became his most absorbing interest and he was an active member of the Dorset Photographic Club. He planned to supply photographs for an illustrated edition of the Wessex Novels, and Thomas Perkins, the Secretary of the Club, introduced Lea to Hardy in order to discuss the project. The plan proved impossible but, with Hardy's assistance, Lea did capture the Wessex countryside as portrayed in the novels and was invited to have the fruit of his labours – *Thomas Hardy's Wessex* (1913) – included in the definitive Wessex edition of Thomas Hardy's works.

Hermann Lea was remembered for his generosity and his unconventionality, for his compassion and his acute observation. He died at Linwood in the New Forest where he had lived for his last thirty years.

The Hardy Guides, Volumes 1 and 2, were first issued as one volume in 1913 and included in the definitive Wessex edition of Thomas Hardy's works. Although this new edition has been prepared with an eye to today's traveller, Hermann Lea's original text has been preserved in its entirety. Any revisions made necessary by changes to the environment are confined to captions. It is remarkable how few such revisions, or revisional captions to Lea's original photographs, have been necessary. Special touring maps have been included to help plan walks and rides through the land described by the original title of Lea's book: *Thomas Hardy's Wessex*.

Hermann Lea

The Hardy Guides
A Guide to the West Country
Volume 2

Edited by Gregory Stevens Cox

Penguin Books

Penguin Books Ltd, Harmondsworth, Middlesex, England
Viking Penguin Inc., 40 West 23rd Street, New York, New York 10010, U.S.A.
Penguin Books Australia Ltd, Ringwood, Victoria, Australia
Penguin Books Canada Limited, 2801 John Street, Markham, Ontario, Canada L3R 1B4
Penguin Books (N.Z.) Ltd, 182-190 Wairau Road, Auckland 10, New Zealand

First published 1986

Conceived and produced by Pilot Productions Limited, 59 Charlotte Street, London

Editorial assistance by Paul Reiderman
Route maps drawn by Rob Shone
Design assistance by Safu Maria Gilbert

Made and printed in Great Britain by Purnell & Sons Limited, Bristol
Duotone reproduction by Anglia Reproductions, Witham, Essex
Typeset in Palatino and Univers by Dorchester Typesetting Limited, Dorchester, Dorset

CONTENTS

The Road to Woodbury Hill

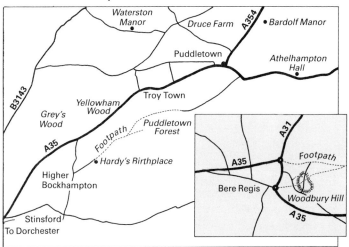

Waterston Manor

Druce Farm

A354

Bardolf Manor

Puddletown

Athelhampton Hall

B3143

Yellowham Wood

Troy Town

Grey's Wood

A35

Footpath

Puddletown Forest

Hardy's Birthplace

Higher Bockhampton

Stinsford
To Dorchester

A31

A35

Footpath

Bere Regis

Woodbury Hill

A35

THE
COUNTRY
OF
"FAR FROM THE MADDING CROWD"

Most of the action in this book takes place in and around the farmstead fictitiously called *Weatherbury Farm*; but before we proceed to that place we will examine the backgrounds which form the setting for the earlier scenes. Our first introduction to Gabriel Oak and Bathsheba Everdene is on the apex of *Norcombe Hill*. We take this to represent Toller Down, where the road to Crewkerne from Dorchester passes through a cutting. It is a spot which figures also [in Volume 1] in the poems, "A Trampwoman's Tragedy" and "The Home-coming," where its natural characteristic of loneliness, tinged with an air of desolation, are further exemplified. "It was a featureless convexity of chalk and soil," we read, – this hill whereon stood Oak's farm – "half-wooded, half-naked . . . covered on its northern side by an ancient and decaying plantation of beeches." Standing 800 feet above the sea, Toller Down lies exposed to the full force of the Atlantic gales, hard to struggle against in autumn and winter when the prevailing wind is westerly.

Our interest soon changes to *Casterbridge*, which we cannot doubt to be drawn in the likeness of Dorchester. It is the date of "the yearly statute or hiring fair," and in imagination we can see the street wherein stand "from two to three hundred blithe and hearty labourers waiting upon Chance." This fair is still held, but year by year it loses its importance, and to-day is little more than a mere gathering of pleasure-seekers, interspersed with a few persons intent on business. We shall probably search in vain for the carter with his emblematic piece of whipcord in his hat; or the thatcher with his "fragment of woven straw"; though the shepherd with his inevitable sheep-crook may be noted occasionally.

We may journey in company with Oak as he walks towards *Shottsford* – an imitation of the town of Blandford. Leaving Dorchester by the London Road, he passes the "water-meadows traversed by little brooks," and at three miles reaches *Yalbury Wood* (Yellowham Wood), ascends the hill of *Yalbury*, and later on comes to *Weatherbury* village. It is then that he notices the fire, and strikes across country to *Weatherbury Farm*. The model which served our author may be found in Waterson House; though to fulfil

Puddletown *(Weatherbury)*
This village was a thriving hive of
agricultural activity in the Victorian
era.

Waterston House *(Weatherbury Farm)*
"A hoary building,of the Jacobean
stage of Classic Renaissance."
The site of *Weatherbury Farm* —
Bathsheba's house in the novel —
is located closer to *Weatherbury*
than Waterston is to Puddletown.
Despite the fire of 1863 much of
the original edifice survives today.

its purpose in the story we must imagine it placed nearer to Puddletown village – for it was Puddletown, in its old guise of fifty or more years ago, which suggested the *Weatherbury* of the Wessex Novels. To be quite exact, however, and to bring the farm and the village into proper focus, we must cut out a section of the country which intervenes between them, to the extent, perhaps, of a mile, or rather more.

Waterson House has suffered from a fire since the date of the story, destroying all the old woodwork; it has moreover passed into other hands quite recently, and extensive alterations are in progress. Nevertheless, we may still trace many of the features described in the book before us. To Oak it showed itself as "a hoary building, of the Jacobean stage of Classic Renaissance"; and we still find the "fluted pilasters" that graced its front, together with the "soft brown mosses, like faded velveteen," patched on its roof.

Little Weatherbury Farm, the imaginary home of Bold-wood, was probably drawn from Druce farmhouse, which stands a full mile nearer Puddletown. A short distance from it is the little cluster of cottages known as Chine Hill, amongst which we notice an old whitewashed house with a thatched roof suggesting *Nest Cottage*, the place where Oak lived after his dismissal from Bathsheba's employment. In the meadow facing this cottage we may find the "sheep-washing pool . . . a perfectly circular basin of brickwork" which served as a theatre for one of the scenes. But the "Great Barn," in which the sheep-shearing was supposed to take place, we shall search for hereabouts in vain. Its "vast porches . . . dusky, filmed, chestnut roof . . . " have either all been swept away, or those features have been imported into the story from a neighbouring place, there being two or three barns in South Dorset of which this would be a faithful description – Cerne Abbas in particular.

We will now turn our attention to *Weatherbury* village. Alas, domestic Puddletown to-day also exhibits little of its old-time characteristics; the site of Warren's Malthouse is now occupied by a neat park fence and shrubbery – and so with most of the other features. Any one entering the well-kept village to-day would grasp little idea of its ancient importance as a small market town. We have it recorded that about the year 1860 Puddletown "contained as many as twenty bootmakers, twelve blacksmiths, twenty carpenters and wheelwrights, five pairs of sawyers, two coopers and some cabinet-makers."[1]

The church, which figures so frequently in the narrative,

[1] From *Memorials of Old Dorset*.

Puddletown Church
(Weatherbury Church)
Troy slept in a porch of
Weatherbury Church on the night
after Fanny Robin's funeral.

Sheep dipping
Sheep dipping is still practised
today in similar fashion (to rid the
animals of parasites).

stands near the square, where in the old days stood the stocks and the court-house (converted later into a private school). This church was one of the finest, interiorly, of any in the county of Dorset, but its recent (1911) alterations, demolitions, and additions have been looked on with dismay by many archaeologists, the late Perpendicular chancel having been converted into a much more spacious new one.

The "little gallery door," through which Troy was supposed to have entered the church, may be seen on the west side of the tower; and we can likewise see the porch in which he is said to have passed the night. The gargoyle, described as "too human to be called a dragon, too impish to be like a man, too animal to be like a fiend, and not enough like a bird to be called a griffin," has been imported from another parish. The huge old elm trees which stood within the churchyard have been felled recently – another matter for regret to those who regard ancient features with respect.

In Troytown, a handful of houses lying at the bottom of *Yalbury Hill*, we recognise "the road-side hamlet called Roy-town." It was once a place of Celtic occupancy, and we may still trace the remains of a miz-maze, or labyrinth, where ancient spectacles were produced. The inn known to us as the *Buck's Head*, the place where Joseph Poorgrass halted with the body of Fanny Robin, was pulled down a few years ago, though it had ceased to be an inn before its demolition.

Several times in the course of the story we are interested in *Casterbridge*. The Corn Exchange was a "low though extensive hall, supported by beams and pillars." If we enter the present building on a market day we shall be struck with the similitude of its human scenes now to what they are described as being then. Here are the farmers with their sample bags of corn, pouring out the contents into their hands – just as we read of Bathsheba doing. We shall, however, look in vain for "the town-bred fowls" who used as a matter of fact to frequent the building in order to pick up the scattered grains.

"The bridge over the Froom" – Grey's Bridge – figures in this story, as well as in so many other of the novels and poems. We see Fanny Robin pausing here to rest on her way to the Union. The other, poorer bridge, at the bottom of the town – Swan Bridge – is where, also in our mind's eye, we see Troy awaiting Fanny and, failing her arrival, journeying to *Budmouth* (approximately Weymouth) to attend the races.

At the "White Hart Tavern," still standing at the lower end of the town, Troy meets Pennyways. The gaol comes

Bath
Where Bathsheba was married.
The famous Roman and Georgian
baths can be visited today.

**The Pleasure Fair, Woodbury
Hill** *(Greenhill)*
"Greenhill was the Nijni Novgorod
of South Wessex." Troy was here
discovered playing Dick Turpin in
a circus act.

The fair was a bustling, hustling
jamboree with everything from
horses to hats, from sheep to
peep shows.

before us when Boldwood goes there to give himself up after shooting Troy. This was, of course, the old building, and must not be taken as identical with the present county gaol.

Yalbury Hill (Yellowham Hill) has been briefly alluded to; it bulks more prominently in "Under the Greenwood Tree" and other of the series; but there are certain references to it in the present volume. As Bathsheba and Troy are slowly driving up the hill from *Casterbridge* Market they meet Fanny, at that hour on her way to the Union Workhouse. Over this hill passes Boldwood as he walks to the gaol.

With *Sherton Abbas* – the imaginatively treated Sherborne – we have little to do here, save that the turnpike house which still stands at the top of the hill leading down into the town marks the spot where Oak and Coggan overtake Bathsheba when she is on her way to Bath to meet Troy.

Bath, according to Cainy Ball, possessed "great glass windows to the shops, and great clouds in the sky, full of rain, and old wooden trees in the country round." Bathsheba was married here, also Lady Constantine in "Two on a Tower" – of which anon.

Lulworth Cove – in the phraseology of our author *Lulstead* or *Lulwind Cove* – is a background for one short scene. Troy reaches this wonderful little basin shut in by rocks the day following his visit to Fanny's grave, and goes out for a swim. We read of his being caught in the current and carried out from the shore. "Far in the distance Budmouth lay upon the sea."

A fresh background comes before us when Bathsheba goes to the fair at *Greenhill*. If we visit Woodbury Hill, close to Bere Regis, on September the 21st, we shall receive an excellent impression of the "Nijni Novgorod of South Wessex." The site marks an ancient British, or Belgic-British, Camp. The fair is said to have been started by a certain packman who, while passing near the hill, was caught in a thunderstorm which drenched him and soaked his pack. After the storm had passed over he climbed over the summit of the hill and spread his cloths and woollens to dry. Some of the villagers from Bere Regis chanced to see the waving cloths and went up out of curiosity, with the result that they promptly purchased all the stock. On that same day in subsequent years the packman again sought the hill-top, having found it such a first-rate market-place; his conduct was followed by other vendors; and in course of time an annual fair grew out of the chance visit. When at its zenith the fair lasted for three weeks, but as markets became more common it gradually declined into a short week, and finally to two days. Once huge flocks of sheep and many cattle and horses changed hands, but to-day there is very little actual business done, and it is little more than a gathering of mere pleasure-seekers. The first day of the fair used to be known as "gentlefolks' day"; the last as "pack-and-penny day." It is here we see Troy again after his temporary exit from the stage; Bathsheba, Boldwood, and many other of our friends are also present; and while on the road homewards Bathsheba is supposed to give Boldwood her conditional promise to marry him.

We should like to find the cottage in which Oak is said to have lived, and where Bathsheba comes to him, but, like so many other cottages of that date, it has disappeared completely.

In a Eweleaze near Weatherbury

There are many spots near Puddletown which might serve for the scenery in this poem, but to those who know the district well it seems to point to a particular grassy down known as Coomb. This field is on the road from Puddletown towards *Egdon Heath*, and was at one time a favourite spot for village festivities.

The Dame of Athelhall

Athelhall is a presentment of Athelhampton, a magnificent example of Tudor building with some evidences of earlier work, and one of the oldest and most beautiful in the county. It is traditionally said to have been erected on the site of a castle, once a stronghold of King Athelstan. In recent years it has been considerably altered and enlarged.

The Dear

"Fairmile Hill-top" is the summit of the hill on the old Sherborne Road from Dorchester, and from it we obtain a wonderful outlook over the southern landscapes. It is said to derive its name from being a fair or full mile long.

THE
COUNTRY
OF

"THE RETURN OF THE NATIVE"

The action of this story is limited to a very circumscribed area, so that the old dramatic quality – unity of place – is deeply marked throughout. The backgrounds are drawn essentially from Nature and few objects of architectural interest intrude. The characters which figure are, with perhaps one exception, entirely in harmony with their environment, and it would be difficult to imagine a more congruous setting for them than that of *Egdon Heath*. This book, which is deemed by some to be Mr. Hardy's masterpiece in prose, gives us convincing proof of our author's appreciation of, and sympathy with, Nature. It is Nature pure, Nature simple, yet illimitable and mysterious.

Egdon Heath represents that vast expanse of moorland which stretches, practically without a break, from Dorchester to Bournemouth. Its natural, untamable wildness is the charm that makes it so subtly attractive, for it defies all attempts at subjugation – except in a few isolated spots, and even then the efforts to cultivate it have involved an amount of labour and expense which is scarcely justified by the results. It is unconquered and unconquerable by agriculture, and more immutable in character than any other part of the Wessex country.

To those who appreciate it, the heath is beautiful at all hours of the day, whether in sunlight or in shade, and at all seasons of the year; but if we would see it in the guise in which it appears in the book before us we must view it at the "transitional point of its nightly roll into darkness"; for we are told "nobody could be said to understand the heath who had not been there at such a time."

As is known to readers, the centre and apex of *Egdon Heath* in the novel is the lofty hill called Rainbarrow. In point of fact the barrow from which this is taken and named is not in the middle of the heath by a long way, but nearly on the western edge. But, apparently to give more of the general effect, it is assumed to be somewhat farther in, at some similar spot where the outlook is more exclusively heathland.

The present writer once spent a night on the barrow, arriving there just before the sun sank behind the tops of *Yalbury Firs*, and watched as "the obscurity in the air and

Bhompston Farm *(Bloom's End)*
The home of Mrs Yeobright,
Tamsin and Clym; now a farm, in
the process of renovation. From
nearby you can take in a
comprehensive view of the
Frome Valley.

A Drive Through the Valley of the Frome and Egdon Heath

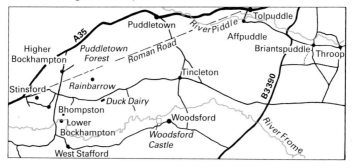

the obscurity in the land closed together in a black fraternization towards which each advanced half-way." It was then that an onlooker could grasp the full significance of its mysterious individuality; could mark how "the place became full of a watchful intentness"; how "the heath appeared slowly to awake and listen." The moon rose from behind the water-meadows that reach out widely on both sides of the river Froom, a creamy light flooding the pool wherein Eustacia Vye was said to have been drowned, gilding the roof-ridge of the *Quiet Woman* Inn, and intensifying "the sombre stretch of rounds and hollows" of which the heath was composed. All was very still, save for the occasional low of a cow from the vale beneath, now wrapped in a winding sheet of white mist. An owl sailed by on muffled wings, silhouetted darkly against the moonlit sky; night-hawks and bats darted hither and thither. Gradually the hours passed, until there seemed to come a struggle on the part of Nature, and an eerie feeling seemed to suggest that "something was about to happen." After a time the tenseness gave place to a sense of relaxation: as though itself sentient, the shadowy heath appeared to be conscious that the strain was past, and the breeze which stole gently out of the flushing east seemed to the watcher like a sigh of relief coming forth from its very core. And behold it was dawn. But long before the faintest glimmer of daylight touched the sky the herons were awake in the fir-clump near by in the direction of peaceful *Blooms-End*; and they screamed harsh, guttural cries as they rose from the trees and flew down into the mist-laden meadows to fish.

Egdon seldom wears the same aspect for long; sensitive to the slightest change of atmospheric influence, it seems to reflect Nature's every mood. In spring the predominant tone is purplish-brown; in summer its purple-red body-colour is patched with green in every conceivable shade; in autumn it displays an orange colour-scheme; while in winter we find russet-browns prevailing, though the heather still carries sufficient purple tinge to be reminiscent of the summer past, and in the hollows the shadows are blue-black and full of lustre.

It does not require a very vivid imagination to picture the effect which *Egdon Heath* must have had on our author when we realise that much of his early life was passed on its very margin; nor can we be surprised that he should have absorbed the atmosphere which belongs to it. The active influence of the heath is marked in many ways by its bearing on the characters. To Eustacia Vye it was a foreign land, for "Budmouth (Weymouth) was her native place, a fashionable seaside resort at that date." To Clym

Egdon Heath
Hardy's fictional name has
become the common
geographical designation for this
tract of land.

Yeobright it was home itself. "Take all the various hates felt by Eustacia Vye towards the heath and translate them into loves, and you have the heart of Clym."

Practically all the incidents take place on *Egdon*; in its wild centre was enacted the mingled tragedy and comedy which made up the lives of the several characters – amid its ancient barrows, its crater-like pits, its rushy pools, under its lichen-shrouded thorns, on its heights, in its valleys. The heath forms a background for many of the scenes in "The Dynasts," "Tess of the d'Urbervilles," "The Fiddler of the Reels," and several pieces of narrative verse.

We will now proceed to explore the heath and view such portions and features as served for the imaginative places described in the book. By taking the London Road out of Dorchester and bearing to the right at the top of Stinsford Hill we shall come, in the course of three miles, to a road turning somewhat abruptly to the left and leading in due course to Puddletown, passing Coomb-Firtrees (see the poem entitled "Yell'ham Wood's Story") on the way. This road strikes us at once as being typical of the "aged highway" along which Captain Vye is supposed to have been walking when he was overtaken by Diggory Venn, the Reddleman. "Before him stretched the long, laborious road, dry, empty, and white. It was quite open to the heath on each side, and bisected that vast dark surface like the parting-line on a head of black hair, diminishing and bending away on the furthest horizon".

It is rare nowadays to meet any one travelling about the country with reddle to sell, but some twenty years ago an occasional vendor might have been seen. Probably the last member of that class is an old woman named Mary-Ann Bull, who, with her ancient pony and still more ancient vehicle, wends her solitary way through Dorset and the adjoining counties, selling silver-sand, peat, reddle, and such-like commodities. Reddle, which is a red chalk, was once extensively used by shepherds for marking their sheep, and at one time farmers were practically dependent on the travelling vendor for their supplies.

The "heath-croppers," those hardy, shaggy animals which drew the Reddleman's van, were once quite common on *Egdon Heath*, but are never seen now, mainly perhaps because many of the ancient common rights have become vested in the lords of the manors.

According to the narrative, the Reddleman had travelled a long distance that day – from *Anglebury*, – which is approximately Wareham – following a road which would have kept him in sight of the heath the whole way. The old road from Wareham to Puddletown crosses the very centre of the *Egdon* expanse, running mostly on the ridge of the

Rainbarrow
"The loftiest ground of the
loneliest height that the heath
contained . . . the pole and axis of
this heathery world." Hardy
"shifted" Rainbarrow to the
centre of his fictional *Egdon*.

hills, with the Froom valley on the left hand and the Pydel valley on the right hand, the latter backed by *Greenhill*– familiar to us in "Far from the Madding Crowd" – Weatherbury Castle, and other landmarks which claim our attention from time to time.

If we will follow Captain Vye and the Reddleman as they pursue their way, we shall see on our left hand the tumuli called Rainbarrows, of which we may consider the largest as representative of the Rainbarrow of the story, although we are inclined to surmise from certain suggestive descriptions that, as we have already hinted, in our author's imagination it stood in a more central portion of *Egdon Heath*; for he says of it: "This bossy projection of earth above its natural level occupied the loftiest ground of the loneliest height that the heath contained. . . . It formed the pole and axis of this heathery world. . . . Above the plain rose the hill, above the hill rose the barrow".

Although the word barrow denotes a mound or hillock in its most literal sense, the term is now employed almost exclusively to signify a burial-place. It was on the top of Rainbarrow that the bonfire was kindled. This method of celebrating historic episodes of the past, which doubtless had its origin in prehistoric times and was directly connected with ceremonies of a religious nature, is now seldom seen. We shall examine the barrow more critically when we come to our chapter on the country of "The Dynasts," where it is again the scene of a fire. The only other illumination which concerns us just now is the little fire supposed to have been lighted by Eustacia Vye on a mound in front of her grandfather's house at *Mistover Knap* – a spot that can be guessed at with some exactitude as being "at the junction of two converging bank fences" to the north of Rainbarrow.

To the group here assembled comes the Reddleman, inquiring his way to *Blooms-End*, and causing consternation by reason of his red attire and his realistic likeness to the "red ghost" seen by the little boy and described by Timothy Fairway. The apparition alarmed Susan Nonsuch also, for she "had a dream last night of a death's-head." This superstitious dread calls to mind an authentic case of an old woman who, when she was a child, used to walk three miles night and morning across the heath to attend school. The only thing she was ever "a-veared o'" was lest "a death's-head" should alight on her and suck her blood! It is obvious that this harmless moth was in her estimation as dangerous as *desmodus rufus*, the blood-sucking bat.

Following the ghosts of the bygone company as they descend to the *Quiet Woman Inn* to "strike up a ballet in front of the married folks' door," we shall find no longer

The Duck Dairy House *(Quiet Woman Inn)*
Only one or two outhouses survive of the original building. This was the inn kept by Damon Wildeve.

an inn but a dairy-house, known to-day as "The Duck."
Once upon a time it was "The Wild Duck Inn," and, earlier
still, "Travellers' Rest," and had a secret hiding-place for
smuggled goods. Two loose floor-boards in the upper
story gave access to a cavity in the walls, undiscernible
from below. The intermediate wall was afterwards removed, but on the ceiling we can still trace the spot where
the opening once was. Evidence of the house having been
an inn originally is shown by a little hatch in the wall
separating the parlour from the kitchen. Through it many
foaming pots of ale used to pass at the time when the story
was written. The *Quiet Woman* figures many times in the
course of the narrative, as also in the short tale entitled
"The Fiddler of the Reels." It should be added that some
features of its description in the novel are borrowed from a
largely similar inn – "The Red Lion," of Winfrith – also
once the haunt of smugglers, and a suggestive spot still.

Mistover Knap was supposed to be only a short distance
from Rainbarrow. Nothing definite remains to mark
where the house originally stood, but we read that close to
it "there was a large pool, bearded all round by heather
and rushes." Such a pool, answering to the description
given, may be found to the north of the barrows, close
under a bank. The remains of an old closed brick-kiln are
in a hollow near. Here our author imagines Eustacia Vye
to have resided – the character described as the "raw
material of a divinity," possessed of "Pagan eyes, full of
nocturnal mysteries." *Mistover* was the fictitious name
given to a few houses which were scattered upon the
heath in this locality; but being built only of mud (*i.e.* clay
mixed with chalk and held together with heather-stems,
tough grasses, straw, etc.), they have completely disappeared. As long as the roof is kept in good repair these
mud-walled houses will last for a long time, but directly
that becomes defective the walls literally melt away. This
method of building is now practically a lost art; very few,
even of the older labourers, possess the requisite know-
ledge and skill. The fir trees which backed the dwelling on
Mistover Knap have likewise disappeared – burned in one
of the fires which ravage the heath at intervals.

Blooms-End, the name given to the home of the Yeo-
brights, was drawn from a farm-house called Bhompston,
which stands in a grass field just off the margin of the
heath in the direction of Lower Bockhampton village. Its
front is much altered now from that of the "irregular,
thatched house" of the story, and the white palings that
once enclosed it have disappeared, but there still remain
certain characteristics, particularly at the back, which will
serve to remind us of the time when the mummers were

Brickyard Cottage *(Alderworth)*
Half a mile to the south of
Briantspuddle lies *Alderworth*, the
home to which Clym took
Eustacia after their marriage.

supposed to have stood in the old oak-beamed room and played "St. George and the Dragon" at the Christmas revels. Mumming, or momming, was common in mediaeval England, and was probably the survival of the Roman masquerade which took place during the orgies of Saturnalia. A spurious imitation, little more than a parody on the original, was occasionally met with a few years back, but the performance was never given with the seriousness usual to it a century or less ago.

There are many curious conical pits on *Egdon Heath*, some being of great depth, and with abrupt, regular sides. A typical one is that known as "Culpepper's Dish," near Briantspuddle, and at no great distance from the cottage which we shall examine later under the name of *Alderworth*. One of these pits forms the background for a short scene when Mrs. Yeobright and Thomasin go to gather holly for the decorations. It was at "the place where the hollies grew, which was in a conical pit, so that the tops of the trees were not much above the general level of the ground." This is a very accurate description of many such pits, and was probably taken from no one in particular.

The church at which Wildeve and Thomasin were supposed to be married may perhaps be regarded as *Mellstock* (Stinsford) – to be referred to more fully in subsequent chapters. It will be remembered that the arrangement to marry at *Anglebury* had fallen through, but on the day newly appointed we see Thomasin setting out to walk to the church, and appearing as "a little figure wending its way between the scratching furze bushes . . ., a pale-blue spot in a vast field of natural brown."

Many of the old-time Wessex customs mentioned in the novels have now become extinct, or nearly so, but one which still flourishes with unabated vigour is the "hair-cutting" referred to in the present story. The Fairways of to-day have altered very little, their methods are still primitive, and almost any Sunday morning we may light upon a similar scene to that described in the book before us. We may then see "the victim sitting on a chopping-block . . . and the neighbours gossiping around." It was at this function that Clym joined the group, and mentioned his determination to "keep a school as near to Egdon as possible."

Another episode which interests us is that of Susan pricking Eustacia with a stocking-needle while in church, on the supposition that she was a witch. This belief in witchcraft will be noticed more fully in a future chapter, where we deal with the story entitled "The Withered Arm." The custom of "blood-drawing" was supposed to constitute the most effective remedy when a person was

Affpuddle *(East Egdon Village)*
The church — still quite unspoilt —
where Clym Yeobright and
Eustacia Vye were married.

"overlooked" by another; and if only the witch's blood could be drawn nothing further need be feared. This practice is resorted to occasionally even now in Wessex, and some authentic instances have come before the present writer within the past few years.

Alderworth is the fictitious name of the cottage which Clym is supposed to have rented after his marriage to Eustacia. It was situated "near a village about five miles off" in the direction of *East Egdon* village. It was at the church in this village that they were married, and we venture to claim it as Affpuddle. *Alderworth* is in a lonely situation; we are told "it was almost as lonely as that of Eustacia's grandfather, but the fact that it stood near a heath was disguised by a belt of firs which almost enclosed the premises." In order to reach it, Clym would have traced backwards for some distance the road by which the Reddleman had reached *Rainbarrow* from *Anglebury*. Through *Stickleford*, under Clyffe Clump – a feature occurring in the poem titled "Yell'ham Wood's Story" – and thence along the old Wareham Road until Moreton North Lodge was reached; from there a turning to the left hand, and a subsequent bearing to the left again, would lead directly to the cottage.

We now read of the "village festivity" to which Eustacia went one afternoon and met Wildeve. He afterwards escorted her homewards as far as Throop Corner, near which place they saw Clym and Diggory Venn. We are unable to locate the actual spot where the dancing took place, but we can readily find Throop Corner – the junction of four cross-roads, of which the northern one leads down the steep declivity into the hamlet of Throop.

Let us follow Mrs. Yeobright as she goes on a broiling day in August to visit Clym at *Alderworth*. "The sun had branded the whole heath with his mark." Tired, weak, often mistaking the way and frequently taking wrong paths, she is presently directed to pursue an individual ahead of her, and whom she at length recognises as her son. She watches him enter the cottage, and then stays to rest awhile under a clump of trees on a knoll; "the place was called the Devil's Bellows." Probably such a knoll existed at the time of the narrative, but we cannot now mark its site with exactness. It was on her return journey that, weak and tired-out, she collapsed and lay on the ground near the path. Here Clym finds her later in the day as he is walking towards *Blooms-End*, and we see him carrying her unconscious form and laying it down in the hut "built of clods and covered with thin turves." She had been bitten on her ankle by an adder, and the remedy suggested by Sam was duly tried. "You must rub the place

The Weir, Woodsford Meadows
(Shadwater Weir)
In a meadow at the back of
Woodsford Castle we can locate
Shadwater Weir, where Eustacia
and Wildeve were drowned.

with the fat of other adders, and the only way to get that is by frying them," he said. But in spite of all their efforts she dies shortly.

This remedy, as our author points out, is a very ancient one. It is still spoken of in Wessex, and occasionally resorted to. Naturally, science of the present day would scoff at such an "old woman's" specific, but nevertheless there are instances on record where it has been known to effect, or aid in, a cure. The separation of mental and physical phenomena cannot be arbitrarily defined, and it is surely not impossible that there may be a material effect in a remedy in which faith plays a prominent part.

A fresh background is before us in the scene of another tragedy. "Shadwater Weir had at its foot a large circular pool, fifty feet in diameter, into which the water flowed through ten large hatches." The actual weir which provided our author with his model may be found in the meadows behind Woodsford Castle, and it can be reached either from that place or by a lane leading from the *Quiet Woman*. It takes the whole water of the river Froom. In summer weather, when the rainfall is low, the water merely glides through the hatches in a calm even stream, the sun shining through the clear water and illuminating the gravelled bottom; but in winter the pool is a boiling cauldron, the flood of water rushes with terrific force, the pool is coated with foam. There has been very little change here since the time when, according to the story, Eustacia Vye was drowned and Wildeve lost his own life in an attempt to rescue her; but probably our author imagined it considerably nearer to the *Quiet Woman* than it actually is.

We read of Diggory Venn's marriage to Thomasin, and their subsequent residence in the dairy at *Stickleford*, a place which may be likened to Tincleton. A visit here will show us a picturesque farm-house of stone, with heavy chimneys, and a general appearance of solidity, which we may surmise served for the dairy-house.

The background for the final scene is again Rainbarrow. Clym is before us – "a motionless figure standing on the top of the tumulus, just as Eustacia had stood on that lonely summit some two years and a half before." And in fancy we can see him there, surrounded by many of his neighbours, who lie at their ease on the heather and listen to the words that fall from his lips. Here he has fixed his pulpit, and his roofless church is typified by the wild expanse of *Egdon Heath*.

By the Barrows

There is a small group of barrows on the heath adjacent to Upper Bockhampton called Rainbarrows, inevitably associated in our minds with "The Dynasts" and "The Return of the Native," but although we recognise and identify these jutting prominences we must not be too literal as regards their position, for it is evident from the descriptions of their environment that in our author's mind they are imagined as standing in a more central portion of the *Egdon* waste. This is so in the poem entitled

The Roman Road

where the line "as the pale parting-line in hair" brings vividly back to us the early chapters of "The Return of the Native," where the same simile is employed. Evidences of this old road are but faintly discernible on the western side of *Egdon Heath*, but when we trace farther eastward – as for instance in the neighbourhood of Wimborne – it betrays itself as a much more clearly marked *via* and approximates closely to the description.

THE
COUNTRY
OF
"THE MAYOR OF CASTERBRIDGE"

As we might expect from the title, the interest of this story centres in *Casterbridge*, a name which we have grown to look on as being synonymous with Dorchester; and it is here, in the capital town of South Wessex, that most of the action takes place. The book before us was first published in volume form in 1886, and it should be noted in passing that the late editions contain nearly a whole chapter more than the first. The story is essentially a biography, the main interest lying around the personality of Michael Henchard, the Mayor.

The surroundings are so graphically and faithfully described that the concrete forms of natural and artificial features which serve as models for the fictitious creations take to themselves the appearance of realities. Some of these, for the more convenient staging of the story, have been tampered with to the extent of moving them a short distance from their actual positions; but this applies only to certain houses, the natural landmarks remain consistently *in situ*. That some of the more ancient houses and other configurations have been altered, demolished, or displaced by more modern structures, is a regrettable fact which the archaeologist must face; though such substitutions would seem to be inseparable from the usual progress of civilisation. Future generations will doubtless realise that these metamorphoses of old towns should be denoted by a term as strong as, or stronger than, vandalism, since the larger proportion are not the outcome of necessity, but the result of a mere destructive policy.

The story opens at *Weydon Priors* – presumably Weyhill – in Upper Wessex, where is enacted the episode of the wife-selling, an incident, it may be mentioned, which is by no means without parallel. The fair is held close to the village of Weyhill. "The spot stretched downward into valleys and onward to other uplands, dotted with barrows and trenched with the remains of prehistoric forts" – a description easily verified to-day. Although a fair is still held there thrice annually, it has steadily declined in magnitude and interest, like all similar institutions; but, nevertheless, Weyhill still holds its record as being the most important sheep-fair in the county, and the visitor to-day may still meet with the "peep-shows, toy-stands,

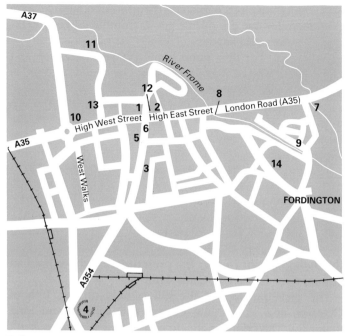

Relive the Casterbridge of Henchard

1 St Peter's
2 Kings Arms
3 Henchard's House
4 Amphitheatre
5 Antelope
6 Cornhill
7 Grey's Bridge
8 The Swan Bridge
9 Mill Street
10 Thomas Hardy Statue
11 The Hangman's Cottage
12 The Corn Exchange
13 Colliton House
14 St Georges

commences his quest we see him entering a church, and there taking a solemn oath to "avoid all strong liquors for the space of twenty years to come." The church in which he registered his oath receives no exact description, and its position can therefore not be pointed out. For many months he pursues his fruitless search, until at last, disappointed, almost despairing of success, he strikes out in a straight line for *Casterbridge*. We may well suppose that the seaport at which he ended his search was Southampton, since we read that "Next day he started, journeying south-westward, and did not pause, except for nights' lodgings, till he reached the town of Casterbridge, in a far distant part of Wessex."

Some sixteen or seventeen years subsequent to this date we are again at the fair of *Weydon Priors*, in company with Henchard's wife and Elizabeth-Jane, but only for quite a short time; they had come to elicit information regarding Henchard's whereabouts, and from the old Furmity Woman they learned that he had left a message with her, in case of inquiries being made, to the effect that "he'd gone to – where? – Casterbridge."

We follow Mrs. Henchard and Elizabeth-Jane as they proceed thither. By walking, and occasionally obtaining a lift in a waggon or carrier's van, they in due course draw near to *Casterbridge*.

It was just before dusk on an evening in mid-September that they paused to rest on the summit of a hill. "The spot commanded a full view of the town and its environs." The vantage point they had reached was assuredly Stinsford Hill – familiar to Hardy readers as *Mellstock Rise*, this name associating it with *Mellstock Village* close by, and the adjacent country inhabited by the members of the *Mellstock Quire*, to whom we are introduced in the book entitled "Under the Greenwood Tree."

To Elizabeth-Jane the town appeared as "an old-fashioned place . . . huddled all together . . . shut in by a square mass of trees, like a plot of garden ground by a box edging." Our author further says of it: "To birds of a more soaring kind, Casterbridge must have appeared on this fine evening as a mosaic work of subdued reds, browns, greys, and crystals, held together by a rectangular frame of deep green," and if we climb to the summit of Stinsford Hill on any clear evening in autumn, we shall be struck with the similitude of the view that stretches before us and the one described. So life-like is the presentment, we can almost persuade ourselves the clock has stood still, that we are living contemporaneously with Henchard, and Farfrae, and Elizabeth-Jane.

Having rested there awhile they went on. "The dense

St Peter's and All Saints' Churches, Dorchester
Lea identifies Hardy's grizzled church whose massive square tower rose unbroken into the darkening sky as the perpendicular church of St Peter, seen here from the east.

trees of the avenue rendered the road dark as a tunnel . . . they passed down a midnight between two gloamings." It must be noted with regret that the fine old elms which formed the avenue on the London Road were broken and uprooted during some of the north-westerly gales about twenty years ago. Younger trees have taken the place of the old, but it will be many years before these will give even an approximate idea of the tunnel-like appearance which it possessed formerly, and which may still be seen exemplified on the Bridport Road as it leaves Dorchester on the western side of the town.

After wandering about the town, here and there, Elizabeth-Jane and her mother sought the High Street. There were "timber houses with overhanging stories . . . there were houses of brick-nogging . . . there were slate roofs patched with tiles, and tile roofs patched with slate, and occasionally a roof of thatch." Instances of these last may still be seen, though most of this wayward, irresponsible architecture has been swept away since the days of Henchard's supposed mayoralty.

Before we follow our characters farther, or identify the places mentioned in connection with them, it may be interesting to glance briefly at the historical associations of the town. The most ancient name by which it was known was *Durnovaria*, clearly of Celtic origin. Its occupation by the Romans would seem to have been a long one, for the whole district teems with relics of Roman buildings, walls, villas, roads, coins, and pottery; but it is generally held that prior to the Roman entry it was a tribal centre of the *Durotriges*, Maiden Castle being regarded as their great stronghold. We have little precise history of Dorchester in Saxon times, when it was called *Dornceaster* or *Dorcestre*, but there is mention of a charter to Milton Abbey, given by Æthelstan in 939, as having come from Doracestria, which at that time purported to be a royal town, and was possessed of a mint. Its present name is of course traceable to the Roman influence. In the year 1613 the town was almost completely destroyed by fire. With some of its later historical connections we shall be concerned presently.

Returning to our wayfarers, we see them standing before "a grizzled church, whose massive square tower rose unbroken into the darkening sky." In this we recognise the Perpendicular Church of St. Peter, from whose belfry the curfew bell still rings, though this is no longer regarded as the signal for shutting the shops! It is said by some archaeologists that St. Peter's Church is built on the site of a Roman Temple. There is some trans-Norman work in the arch spanning the door of the south porch. Inside are some interesting effigies; the Hardy

Barclay's Bank, South Street, Dorchester *(Henchard's House, Casterbridge)*
On 1 March, 1904, Hardy wrote to Lea: "The view of Henchard's house which you propose to take will, I fear, make a prosaic picture, being a flat front elevation; unless you could do it aslant from some upper window on the other side of the street." The building was once the home of Giles Symonds who, it has been argued, served as the model for *Henchard*.

The King's Arms Hotel *(King's Arms Hotel, Casterbridge)*
The exterior remains virtually unchanged since Hardy described it in the nineteenth century. It was here that the dinner was held at which we encounter Henchard in his role as the Mayor of Casterbridge.

The Almshouse *(Napier's or Nappers Mite, South Street)*
The building has survived to house a cafe and offices.

Chapel at the end of the south aisle brings back to us forcibly our author's connection with the town through his ancestors. In the close will be seen the bronze statue erected to the memory of William Barnes.

"Other clocks struck eight from time to time; one gloomily from the gaol, another from the 'gable of an almshouse. . . .'" The gaol, which interests us more particularly in the story entitled "The Withered Arm," stands on the site once occupied by a Norman Castle, of which we find mention in records of the twelfth and thirteenth centuries. The short, steep hill which ascends from the river is called Castle Hill to-day. The Almshouse is doubtless the one in South Street, known as Napier's or Napper's Mite.

Our next halt is in front of the King's Arms Hotel (figuring under its rightful name). Its "spacious bow-window projected into the street over the main portico," and does so still. Here Farfrae comes on the scene, and in reply to his inquiry for "a respectable hotel . . . more moderate than this," he is recommended to "The Three Mariners, just below." This hostel, with its "two prominent gables, bow-window, and passage light," has been pulled down since the book was written, but certain features may still be traced in the "four-centred Tudor arch" which leads into the stable-yard.

Passing up the High Street the day following, Elizabeth-Jane took notice of the carriers' vans which hailed "from Mellstock (Bockhampton), Weatherbury (Puddletown), The Hintocks (Minterne, etc.), Sherton Abbas (Sherborne), Kingsbere (Bere Regis), Overcombe (partly Upwey), and many other towns and villages round." These vans form a particularly noticeable feature in Dorchester, and may also be seen in Salisbury and many other ancient market towns in Wessex. But the penned pigs and the rows of horses no longer fill the High Street on fair-days, and must be sought for in the market field.

The house in which Henchard lived was, we read, "one of the best, faced with dull red and grey old brick". Such a house may be seen in South Street, standing a little back from the pavement, its rear pointing towards *Durnover* (supposititiously Fordington), where stood the barns and granaries which pertained to the corn merchant's trade. Just previous to Elizabeth's visit there to find Henchard, we see him, in company with Farfrae, passing up the High Street to Top o' Town, bearing suddenly to the right, and turning "down an avenue on the town wall called Chalk Walk (probably Colliton Walk), leading to an angle where the north and west escarpments met". These walks are in reality boulevards, being placed exactly on the top of the

The Amphitheatre, Dorchester
(Casterbridge)
"The Amphitheatre was to
Casterbridge what the Coliseum
is to modern Rome and nearly of
the same magnitude." Hardy
himself came across Roman
remains when his house – Max
Gate – was being constructed on
the outskirts of Dorchester in the
1880's.

Walks, Dorchester *[Casterbridge
Walks]*
Lea took several photographs of
the Walks in Dorchester. This
particular picture carries Hardy's
own pencilled recommendation
for possible use: "Good as a
photograph [& might be
substituted for West Walk] if that
should fail."

actual earthen vallum thrown up by the Romans when they fortified the town. As late as the end of the eighteenth century considerable lengths of the Roman stone wall were found. On the east the great walls were actually grubbed up, partly because they formed an obstruction, and partly in order that the avenues of trees might be planted thereon.

Our next background is the place where Henchard agreed to meet his wife. "The Ring at Casterbridge" was merely the local name of one of the finest Roman Amphitheatres, if not the very finest, remaining in Britain". In the Wessex poem entitled "Her Death and After" it is referred to as the *Cirque of the Gladiators*. At this point in the narrative we are reminded of the tremendous influence the Roman occupation had on Dorchester. "Casterbridge announced old Rome in every street, alley, and precinct. It looked Roman, bespoke the art of Rome, concealed dead men of Rome." The building of Mr. Hardy's house at Max Gate brought to light many Roman relics, including several ancient graves in which were coins, pottery, urns, etc. Maumbury Rings is an alternative title by which the Amphitheatre is known – a name connected perhaps with the word mummery. Recent excavations have brought to light many interesting points in connection with its origin and its purpose: an account of these researches may be obtained from the County Museum at Dorchester. It was here, at this spot so charged with ancient reminiscences, that the husband and wife were said to meet after dusk had fallen, and at the end of their interview Henchard recommended Susan to take lodgings for the time being "over the china shop in High Street." We may find this house almost opposite the County Museum, joining to the house as Judge Jeffreys' Lodgings – the place where he lodged during the Bloody Assizes. The lower part is still used as a china shop. The Amphitheatre also serves as a meeting-place for Henchard and Lucetta later on in the narrative.

At the date of the story, Dorchester was enclosed in a much more restricted area, the streets were narrower, the houses were more tightly packed. It was "a place deposited in a block upon a corn-field." At that time Fordington appears to have been the centre of the agricultural interests, for we read that "wheat ricks overhung the old Roman street and thrust their eaves against the church tower; green thatched barns, with doorways as high as the gates of Solomon's temple, opened directly upon the main thoroughfare." It was in one of these granaries on *Durnover Hill* (Fordington Hill), situated at the back of Henchard's house, and close to the

South Street, Dorchester
(Casterbridge)
Hardy worked in an architect's
office in South Street for a while,
in the heart of what became his
Wessex.

church, that Elizabeth-Jane's meeting with Farfrae is described. The "humpbacked barn, cushioned with moss, and the granary, rising against the church tower behind," have disappeared completely. They were demolished in order to make room for the new rectory, and also because they stood so close to the church as to throw an awkward shade and darken the windows.

The Antelope Hotel (known by its real name) is an interesting old hostel of the seventeenth century, to be found on the side of South Street opposite to where Henchard's house stands, but a little nearer Cornhill. It interests us only as being the place appointed by Lucetta for her first interview with Henchard.

If we continue to follow the events in the order related, we shall now find ourselves confronted with the rival entertainments of Henchard and Farfrae. "Close to the town was an elevated green spot surrounded by an ancient square earthwork." This was *Pummery* or Poundbury, and represented the site chosen by Henchard as being a suitable spot for his merry-making. There is much controversy regarding the origin of this earthwork, antiquarian experts placing it as British, Roman, Danish – according to individual conviction; while others hold that it probably partakes of all three epochs and was severally occupied and altered at three distinct periods. It lies just outside the town to the north-west. Farfrae's opposition fête was held in the West Walks – still so called. At its termination we see Farfrae escorting Elizabeth-Jane home, passing "down the West Walk, and then into the Bowling Walk," and thus up South Street. Bowling Walk is another of the features that shows under the same title to-day.

The *Corn Market* – a place which figures conspicuously in "Far from the Madding Crowd" – is also frequently mentioned here. At the time when Henchard was ostensibly mayor, this particular section of the town wore a very different aspect. The roadway passing between the present corn exchange and St. Peter's Church was at that time spanned by an arch connecting the two buildings. *Bullstake Square* (North Square), to which the arch gave entrance, had a stone post in its centre, and to it the bull was tied for baiting. Bull-baiting, it may be noted, was only put a stop to by Act of Parliament in 1835. Here, too, were the stocks – now reposing in the County Museum – and likewise the old town pump which now stands in Cornhill. In the story this formed a favourite meeting-place for Mother Cuxsom, Solomon Longways, and the other gossips of the town.

After the death of Mrs. Henchard, and the reading of the letter of confession which she left behind her, we see her

Colliton House *(High Place Hall)*
This, the residence of Lucetta, today houses the offices of the County Council. The arch and mask – "one of its most curious and interesting features", according to Lea – can be found decorating the doorway to the library of the County Museum.

Fordington Church *(Durnover Church)*
The last 200 years have seen much alteration to the building. It was Hardy himself who designed the Gothic pillars in the north aisle. The thatched wall, promenade and many of the tombstones are quite gone today.

The Friary Mill
The mill no longer stands today.

husband in a morbid frame of mind leaving the house and passing down the street until he reaches a bridge. Thence he follows the path beside the river. "These precincts embodied the mournful phases of Casterbridge life. . . . Here were ruins of a Franciscan Priory." In the darkness, passing the old County gaol – not to be confounded with the present building – with the sound of the roaring weir in his ears and his mind full of unrest, he reaches the cottage where the local hangman lived, climbs up the steep hill called Glydepath Rise, and re-enters the town.

All this part of Dorchester is naturally much altered since the date assumed for the story, but we may still see sufficient realism to bring the scene back to our minds. The old brick bridge, from which the pathway leads, will be referred to later on. Friary Mill, once attached to the Franciscan Priory, still exhibits a certain picturesqueness, though modern disregard for the beautiful in favour of the merely utilitarian has denuded it of many old salient features. It is supposed to stand close to the site of a Norman castle and to be built partly out of the stones that once formed the castle walls.

A little beyond the mill is a deep hole, darkly shadowed by willow trees; this we may regard as the place "wherein nameless infants had been used to disappear". Still following the river path and passing the present gaol, we soon see before us a picturesque thatched cottage, still known as the hangman's cottage. But as this bulks more largely in the short story entitled "The Withered Arm" we shall examine it more closely in a later chapter. Close beside it is a weir over which the water pours with considerable force, emitting the roar which assailed Henchard's ears.

On *Durnover Hill* (Fordington Hill) we come upon the cemetery in which it is alleged Susan Henchard was interred – "a churchyard old as civilisation. . . . Mrs. Henchard's dust mingled with the dust of women who lay ornamented with glass hairpins and amber necklaces, and men who held in their mouths coins of Hadrian, Posthumus, and the Constantines," says our author, thus reminding us again of the Roman connection with Dorchester. Some late alterations to Fordington Church have disclosed a stone slab bearing the names of certain Roman citizens carved in Roman type. It was here that Elizabeth-Jane supposedly came to visit her mother's grave, and made her first acquaintance with Lucetta.

High Place Hall, the residence of Lucetta, was apparently drawn from Colliton House. Its actual position, however, must be imagined farther eastwards, towards North Square. "The Hall, with its grey *façade* and parapet . . . was

Mill Street (*Mixen Lane*)
"This mildewed leaf in the sturdy
and flourishing Casterbridge plant
..." Even in Lea's day many of
the houses in this area of
Dorchester had been cleared;
today there is no evidence of its
erstwhile notoriety.

entirely of stone . . . its rooms overlooked the market-place. . . ." One of its most curious and interesting features is the bricked-up doorway in the wall and the mask which adorns the keystone. "Originally the mask had exhibited a comic leer, as could still be discovered; but generations of Casterbridge boys had thrown stones at the mask, aiming at its open mouth, and the blows thereof had chipped off the lips and jaws as if they had been eaten away by disease." In this house Elizabeth-Jane is said to take up her residence, and many interesting scenes are staged within its walls and in the market-place which its windows overlooked. The Museum, to which she was sent by Lucetta soon after her arrival, was "an old house in a back street. There are crowds' of interesting things – skeletons, teeth, old pots and pans, ancient boots and shoes, birds' eggs – all charmingly instructive." The place mentioned must not be confounded with the present County Museum, but must be sought for in a house in Trinity Street, adjacent to the stable-yard of the Antelope Hotel.

Lucetta's visit to *Port-Bredy* (Bridport) leads directly to the scene in the barn on the Bridport Road. It is known as Damer's Barn, and it lies in the dip of the hill just at the end of the west avenue. "The spot was a vale between two gentle acclivities, and the road, still adhering to its Roman foundation, stretched onward straight as a surveyor's line till lost to sight on the most distant ridge," – a statement verified by a visit to-day.

Our interest is now claimed by those portions of *Casterbridge* which were said to be frequented by the less prosperous inhabitants. "Two bridges stood near the lower part of Casterbridge town. The first, of weather-stained brick, was immediately at the end of High Street (the eastern extremity). . . . The second bridge, of stone, was farther out on the highway". The description given in the book is as true to-day as when it was written. An examination of the actual fabric discloses the evidence of that peculiar wear and tear due to the unconscious leanings and rubbings and heel-friction; while the persons who are to be seen lounging against the parapets seem still to resemble the types referred to in a marked degree. With the habitués of the brick-built bridge – that one just at the bottom of the town – must be included those "of the lowest character." On the stone bridge – Grey's Bridge, farther down the London Road – we find a different set of loiterers: "the miserables who would pause on the remoter bridge were of a politer stamp. They included bankrupts, hypochondriacs . . . shabby-genteel men." These bridges are important features and receive

The Swan Bridge and Grey's Bridge, Dorchester
(The Two Bridges, Casterbridge)

"There was a marked difference of quality between the personages who haunted the near bridge of brick [The Swan Bridge] and the personages who haunted the far one of stone. Those of the lowest character preferred the former, adjoining the town; they did not mind the glare of the public eye. They had been of comparatively no account during their success; and, though they might feel dispirited, they had no particular sense of shame in their ruin . . . Instead of sighing at their adversities, they spat; and instead of saying the iron had entered into their souls, they said they were down on their luck . . . The *misérables* who would pause on the remoter bridge [Grey's Bridge] were of a politer stamp. They included bankrupts, hypochondriacs, persons who were what is called 'out of a situation' from fault or lucklessness, the inefficient of the professional class . . . The eyes of this species were mostly directed over the parapet upon the running water below."

mention in several of the novels and poems.

To those who love realism for its own sake, *Mixen Lane* (Mill Street) will come as a disappointment. Even at the time when the story was written this section of *Casterbridge* was in a stage of transition, and to-day there only remain slight indications of its original sordid character. Many of the houses have been pulled down, condemned as unfit for human habitation; the moral atmosphere has to a large extent been similarly purged, and a special mission has lately been inaugurated, having for its object the cleansing of this Augean Stable. "Mixen Lane was the Adullam of all the surrounding villages. . . . The Inn called Peter's Finger was the church of Mixen Lane." This inn has been demolished, like so many of the houses in Mill Street. Its name may be found in the inn at Lytchett Minster – a building figuring in "The Hand of Ethelberta" – where the hanging sign is supposedly a portrait of *St. Peter ad Vincula*. It is here, in *Mixen Lane*, we are introduced to some of the shadier characters which form the appendages to Henchard. Jopp, the Furmity Woman, Mother Cuxsom, Nance Mockridge – all had their residences around the inn, and it was inside this little hostel that "the skimmity ride" was planned. This curious custom is now extinct, but the present writer can remember such a function taking place in more than one village near Dorchester within the last twenty-five years, and many people are still alive who have actually taken a part in the processions. The result of the "skimmity ride" was even greater than the originators had planned, Lucetta – now Mrs. Farfrae – being stricken down by the shock and expiring shortly after the procession had passed beneath her window. It was after learning of her seizure that Henchard set off to try to find Farfrae and expedite his return. We see him hastening through the town, crossing *Durnover Moor*, and climbing *Mellstock Hill*, until he reaches *Yalbury Bottom* – the base of Yellowham Hill – and instead of going straight home, proceeding up Cuckoo Lane to *Mellstock Village* (Lower Bockhampton).

Later on, as will be remembered by readers, Henchard contemplates suicide, and proceeds to *Ten Hatches Hole* for that purpose. We can see the Ten Hatches from Grey's Bridge, on the northern side of the road, and we can reach the spot by following the path which runs alongside the river. Here he discovers his effigy "in the circular pool formed by the wash of centuries – the pool he was intending to make his death-bed," and his purpose is frustrated thereby, for he superstitiously takes the effigy to be his real self. *Ten Hatches Hole* is also a feature in the poem entitled "The Curate's Kindness".

**Damer's Barn, the Bridport
Road, Dorchester** *(Casterbridge)*
Unfortunately, Hardy's statement
is no longer verifiable, the "vale
between the two gentle
acclivities" having been
developed as a residential area.

We should like to identify the Corn Store near *Durnover* Church, where Henchard is supposed to have lived for a while with Elizabeth-Jane, but it has been entirely swept away. It was about this time that we read: "Elizabeth . . . often took her walks on the Budmouth (Weymouth) Road. . . . A quarter of a mile from the highway was the prehistoric fort called Mai Dun, of huge dimensions and many ramparts. . . ." We are told that Henchard often went there to watch for her appearance on the highway. This huge earthwork, which is the finest in the country, forms a feature in one of the poems and will be referred to in a later section of this book. The remaining, and perhaps the saddest, part of Henchard's career it is only necessary to recapitulate briefly. After learning of Elizabeth-Jane's determination to marry Farfrae he decides to leave *Casterbridge* and sets out at dusk, with his tool-basket slung over his shoulder and clad in his old working clothes. Elizabeth-Jane accompanies him as far as "the second bridge on the highway" – Grey's Bridge. In due course he reaches *Weydon Priors*. Here, on "the renowned hill," he mentally reconstructs the scene of his first visit, but soon the attraction of *Casterbridge*, due to his affection for Elizabeth-Jane, draws him in that direction, and we read of him circling the town, though still at some distance from it. For a time he pursues his old work of hay-trussing, labouring on a farm "near the old Western Highway," until, chancing to learn the date of the forthcoming wedding, he strikes out in a bee-line for *Casterbridge*. The second night of his journey he stops at *Shottsford* – suggestive of Blandford – where he purchases a goldfinch to take to Elizabeth-Jane as a wedding gift. At noon the next day he reaches the top of *Yalbury Hill* (Yellowham Hill), where comes to his ears "the soft pealing of the Casterbridge bells . . . a signal that all had gone well".

Next we see him at his old home, watching the dancing. His disappointment with life seemed now to reach its culminating point, and the tragedy of it pours in on his consciousness with overwhelming force, so that he turns his back on *Casterbridge* for ever.

In his track, along the *Melchester* (Salisbury) highway eastward, press Farfrae and Elizabeth-Jane, diverging from the Salisbury Road at "Weatherbury (Puddletown) by a forking highway which skirted the north of Egdon Heath." *Egdon Heath* concerns us in "The Return of the Native," and elsewhere, and it will suffice here to remark that this stretch of country extends practically from Dorchester to Bournemouth. "They searched Egdon, but found no Henchard." They continue to search for him

The Phoenix Hotel, Dorchester
(Casterbridge)
No longer a tavern, but the sign
outside what is now a shop tells
of the building's original function.

until they reach an "extension of the heath to the north of Anglebury (Wareham)." Here, in a cottage "built of kneaded clay," they find Henchard's body. The cottage has doubtless long passed away; the actual clump of fir trees has not disappeared; from the description we may gather that it stands on one of the highest points of Corfe Mullin heath, some twenty miles distant from Henchard's old home at *Casterbridge*.

The Burghers

We find the scene laid in Dorchester, the *Casterbridge* of the novels. Here, in the old High Street, the friends are supposed to meet. The hour is aptly determined by the words:

The sun had wheeled from Grey's to Dammer's Crest;

that is to say, from Grey's Bridge or Grey's Wood to the eastward, very familiar to us in "Under the Greenwood Tree," to the apex of Damer's Hill, which lies just outside the town on the Bridport Road, close to the barn which we inspected in "The Mayor of Casterbridge." The house described as the "Pleasaunce hard by Glyd'path Rise" is the same house which we have ascribed to Lucetta in the last-mentioned book, and known to-day as Colliton House. "Three hours past curfew" fixes the point of time with accuracy, for St. Peter's Church still announces the curfew nightly at eight o'clock.

In imagination we pass down the High Street in the still hours when the town is wrapped in sleep, and turn down the narrow road called Glyde Path Road. Before us stands Colliton House, looking grey and ghastly in the faint light, and close beside it the ancient gateway with the grinning mask forming its keystone. To appreciate fully the depth and feeling of the poem we need to visit the scene at such an hour, to view it by the faint light of the stars, rather than by the strenuous light of the sun.

Her Death and After

Here we are still in *Casterbridge*. Right at the top of High West Street, facing directly down the street, is a solidly built house known as Top o' Town. It was from this house that "her tenement" was drawn. The *Western Wall* has received mention in "The Mayor of Casterbridge," where it is called *Chalk Walk* – another less-used name for Colliton Walk. In the *Field of the Tombs* we recognise the cemetery on the Weymouth Road – just beyond the *Cirque of the Gladiators*, or Maumbury Rings, lately examined by the antiquaries.

The Barracks, Dorchester
(Casterbridge)
Dorchester, a garrison town, was
quarters for many a *"war-torn
stranger"*.

The Dance at the Phoenix

The "Phoenix" is one of the old-time hostelries of Dorchester (though with a new frontage) and stands in High East Street, nearly opposite the "Three Mariners" – a familiar spot in "The Mayor of Casterbridge". "The Faynix" has always been favoured by the soldiery at the barracks for their convivial gatherings. Various other features mentioned in this poem have also come before us in the last-named book, but *Standfast Bridge* occurs here for the first time. We shall find it passing down the length of Mill Street.

Casterbridge Captains

Here we need only visit the church of All Saints, to which our author refers in "the ancient aisle." The names said to be carved on the seat-back were there before the reseating, and at this distance of time there may be no harm in giving them as J. B. Lock, T. G. Besant, and J. Logan.

The Revisitation

In this poem we can follow mentally in the tread of the restless sojourner as he passes under the gateway of the barracks at *Casterbridge*, and, descending the High Street, walks over the "battered bridge." We have many times followed this route, particularly when we were examining the surroundings in "The Mayor of Casterbridge," where this bridge – Grey's Bridge – also figured. Dorchester has of course altered very considerably since the 'forties, when Henchard was imagined as Mayor, but even to-day we may obtain some idea of *Old Casterbridge* if we view it at night, when folk are abed and asleep and our footsteps echo noisily on the worn flagstones of the High Street. Grey's Bridge, built 1748, teems with associations; it frequently becomes the "Bridge of Sighs" in the Wessex Novels and Poems, for it has figured many times as the spot where those oppressed in spirit paused to contemplate the alternative to continued existence.

Crossing the bridge, the solitary man continues up the "lonely Lane of Slyre" towards Waterstone Ridge. This road, too, we have travelled, when we journeyed with Burthen in his carrier's van towards *Longpuddle*. But when we reach the apex of the long incline we leave the high road, to enter the "downland thinly grassed," where we come upon the barrows – "immemorial funeral piles" – scattered here and there, some showing their ancient shape, others wellnigh levelled with the ground. If we search diligently we can find a boundary-stone of some size, now half-buried and overgrown, but undoubtedly

The Manor-House, Muston
Agnette lived "below there in the Vale . . . the downlands were her father's fief" and Lea gives her residence as the "old farmstead called Muston, once a manor-house".

Ten Hatches *(Ten Hatches Hole)*
"The river here ran deep and strong at all times." Today only five of the hatches remain at the spot where Henchard contemplated suicide.

deserving the title of "sarsen." Where it originally came from we can only conjecture – perhaps from the Wiltshire downs, where the hill-sides and valleys are thick with them, and where they have earned the name of "the grey wethers" from their suggestive likeness to sheep lying at rest.

The wayfarer's visitant lived "below there in the Vale," and we may like to picture her residence as the old farmstead called Muston, once a manor-house. He wakes when the sun is rising, when it blazed from "the Milton Woods to Dole-hill" – two prominences which rear themselves out of the vale to the north-east and north, and which can be readily distinguished from this spot. And then in fancy we see him retracing his steps, descending the hill, recrossing the "battered bridge," and entering the gateway of the barracks.

Bereft

The *Casterbridge* features here brought to our notice have already been examined. *Durnover Lea* is more or less akin to Fordington Moor; while Grey's Bridge has been identified many times.

The Curate's Kindness

It was at *Pummery*, or else at *Ten-hatches Weir*, that the misogynist of this ironical poem thought to end his forty years of matrimonial infelicity. *Pummery*, or Poundbury, weir is a deep dark silent pool in fair weather, and a raging torrent after rain. It lies snugly under the escarpments of Poundbury Camp and is reached most easily from the Sherborne road out of Dorchester. Ten-hatches is the weir in the Froom meadows, in sight of Grey's Bridge, and is familiar to us as the hole wherein Henchard, in "The Mayor of Casterbridge," is imagined to have watched his effigy floating on the morning following the skimmity ride.

A Wife Waits

We are still in the vortex of the Dorchester of olden times. *Cornmarket Place, The Cross, The White Hart, Grey's Bridge,* and the *High Street* – all these we have already explored; *Clock-corner steps* is the only feature foreign to us, and this spot has been altered too completely to allow us to trace any points of similarity between it and the steps which now lead into the Corn Exchange.

After the Fair

The "Club-room" mentioned here has been swept away. It stood once facing on to North Square, better known to

Hardy readers as *Bull-stake Square,* in which guise it comes before us repeatedly in "The Mayor of Casterbridge." We read in a footnote that "The Bow (where the wife waited) . . . is not now so described," but, thanks to the present Curator of the County Museum, the old name has been replaced.

THE
COUNTRY
OF

"UNDER THE GREENWOOD TREE"

This story deals with a phase of rural life which is now unfortunately extinct. A quarter of a century ago a string-choir might still be heard occasionally in some of the village churches in Wessex, but the only instances to-day are where certain vicars have endeavoured to revive the string-music for some special service – a proceeding which has not always proved to be the success anticipated. In the preface to the last edition of this novel we find some interesting details about the players: "Their music in those days was all in their own manuscript, copied in the evenings after work, and their music-books were home-bound." Some of the instruments were actually made by the players themselves. Here are facts which show us how strong was the interest taken in their work by the musicians: they had then a prescriptive interest in the services; the instruments and the music-books were handed down from father to son through many generations. Whilst earnestly determined to do their duty to the church in which they performed, they nevertheless found ample leisure to play tricks on one another. There is an authentic story told of two brothers, one of whom accused the other of "blowin' too harrd an' dhrownin' t'others' instruments." But as the recipient of the accusation stoutly denied the imputation, and refused to moderate his vigorous performance, the brother packed his flute with paper in such a manner as to leave only one note open, and the player, blissfully unconscious, continued to follow the score with unabated zeal!

The present writer has seen and handled some of the home-made instruments, as well as several of the manuscript music-books. The latter often contain a curious mixture of carols, secular songs, psalms, and quaint ditties more suitable to Christmas revelry than church worship. The accompanying illustration is reproduced from a manuscript music-book which once belonged to a noted member of the *Mellstock Quire*[1]. It may not be necessary to remind readers that, until the end of the seventeenth century, this word was written as pronounced, viz. Quire, a spelling still retained in the Book of Common Prayer.

[1] The circular mark on the right-hand page is a stain resulting from the wet base of a cider mug.

Mellstock Cross
To be found 2 miles out of Dorchester on the road to Tincleton. "The hamlets on either side of us are the Mellstock villages."

A manuscript music-book which belonged to a member of the Mellstock Quire (a spelling of "choir" used up to the end of the seventeenth century).

Stinsford Vicarage (Mellstock)
The last call of the night for the Mellstock choir.

The story is laid in or about the year 1840 – a date which the "ecclesiastical bandsmen" played in many churches in the neighbourhood of *Mellstock*.

In tracing the backgrounds which figure in this book we find ourselves concerned with localities rather than with buildings, for with few exceptions these have been swept away or so completely altered as to render recognition impossible. The fictitious name of *Mellstock* included the several villages, hamlets, and isolated houses comprised in the parish of Stinsford. Upper and Lower Bockhampton, Stinsford House and cottages, Kingston Maurward, Bhompston and Higher Kingston may all be regarded as suggestively comprehended in the general name.

Mellstock Lane is the road leading northwards from *Mellstock Cross* – the right-angled roads which intersect about two miles from Dorchester on the Tincleton road. Here we are introduced to the members of the choir, who are supposed to be on their way to Dick Dewy's house at *Upper Mellstock* – a place which seems to us to be typical of Upper Bockhampton. As they journey thither they soon see "glimmering indications of the few cottages forming the small hamlet." If we are correct in our surmise, we shall easily find the little hamlet; the tranter's house, however, has disappeared. It was as composite picture, drawn from two models, one of which is no longer in existence, while the other has been so much altered as to show no resemblance to "the long low cottage with a hipped roof of thatch" familiarised to us in the story.

If we follow the choir when, having first refreshed themselves with the tranter's cider – made probably from a purely local apple, the "Bock'a'ton Sweet" (Bock'a'ton being a corruption of Bockhampton), – they make a start for the "outlying homesteads and hamlets," we are led to the school-house at *Lower Mellstock* – a place approximately closely to Lower Bockhampton. The present school-house may have been built since the date of the story, though it bears no great unlikeness to the building from which the *Mellstock* school-house was drawn.

The next house to be visited is Farmer Shiner's, and we may discover its prototype in the house standing above the bridge at the bottom of the village, nowadays more enclosed than formerly.

We now see them crossing *Mellstock Bridge* and going along "an embowered path beside the Froom" on their way to the church and vicarage. The pathway interests us more particularly as one of the features in the mystic poem entitled "The Dead Quire". As we pass along it we catch a glimpse through the trees of the *Knapwater House* which figures in "Desperate Remedies." The call at the vicarage –

**The Bridge and Riverside
House, Lower Bockhampton**
(Mellstock Village)

**The Keeper's Cottage,
Yellowham Wood** *(Yalbury)*
A little off the A35, the
Puddletown to Dorchester road,
in the wood on Yellowham Hill lies
the Keeper's cottage.

suggested by the house standing close to Stinsford Church – is the last for that night, and the respective members of the choir soon disperse and go homewards.

The next scene is supposed to take place in *Mellstock* – presumably Stinsford – Church. This church has been twice restored of late years and the old musicians' gallery removed. It contains some interesting monuments to the Pitt family, also a brass tablet to the memory of some Hardys of our author's family who are buried here. The piers of the "north gate or 'church hatch'" are crowned with two large decorated urns. It is with the old gallery that we are particularly concerned. It had "a status and sentiment of its own," we are told; and we can readily credit the relative ecclesiastical grades of those who occupied it and those who sat in the body of the church. "The nave knew nothing of the gallery people, as gallery people, beyond their loud-sounding minims and chest notes."

The workshop of Mr. Penny stood, we are told, in "the lower village." We cannot trace such a place there now, but from one of the older residents we can hear of just such a workshop having been there long ago and we have seen a water-colour of the same.

Yellowham Wood, in its imaginary name of *Yalbury Wood*, is the background for the scene when Dick goes, with "Smart the mare and the light spring-cart," to fetch Fancy from her father's house. This wood figures several times in the Novels and in the Poems. It is about half-way between Dorchester and Puddletown. The keeper's cottage – now remodelled – which was imagined as her home, lies a little off the road; it is reached by a drove turning off just at the bottom of the hill on the Dorchester side. Its principal feature in our author's mind seems to have been the huge "chimney-corner" – for which we shall, however, look in vain. Its original size may be surmised from the information given us that it was large enough to contain, "in addition to Geoffrey himself, Geoffrey's wife, her chair, and her work-table, entirely within the line of the mantel, without danger or even inconvenience from the heat of the fire." Occasional instances of these cavernous chimney-corners, quite common in our author's youth, are to be met with still, but they become rarer year by year.

The action now turns for a short time to *Budmouth* – the name under which Weymouth passes in the Wessex Novels. It forms an important stage for some scenes in "The Dynasts," and occurs frequently in "The Trumpet-Major." Dick is assumed to have gone there with some swarms of bees for Mr. Maybold's mother and to have met

Upper Bockhampton

Hardy wrote to Lea: "In case you should be thinking of giving a view of spots in Upper Bockhampton . . . there are reasons against it – not least being the nuisance occasioned to those who live there by trippers with Kodaks looking over hedges." Understandable sentiments from the village's most famous son, but three days later he relented, explaining that his reticence was due "to an experience I had had a few days earlier, when, on a private walk to the house in question, I was, unknown to myself, kodaked by some young men who were on the watch."

The Ship Inn, Upwey

At the foot of Ridgeway hill, we find the Ship little altered today, although the old ship's mast, which displayed its sign in Hardy's day, has been replaced.

Fancy at "the corner of Mary Street . . . near the King's statue." We see them in imagination as they drive homewards together to *Mellstock*. The road passes through Upwey, and just at the foot of Ridgeway Hill stands the inn called "The Ship", where we are told they stopped to have tea and rest the horse. This appears to have been a momentous tea-drinking, for by and by "the newly-affianced youth and maiden passed up the steep hill to the Ridgeway, and vanished in the direction of *Mellstock*."

At the highest point in Upper Bockhampton, just where *Egdon Heath* commences, there is a wood on the left-hand side through which a drive has been cut. If we follow this track it will bring us out into the high road leading from Dorchester to Puddletown. Just opposite is another gate, giving into a further section of the same wood, and in which a similar pathway will be found. This we may recognise as the "Snail-Creep" – still its name – the path followed by Dick when he went nutting in Grey's Wood. He had reached it by way of Cuckoo Lane – the northern section of the track known in this novel as *Mellstock Lane*. As he is returning homewards, and just as he has "passed over a ridge which rose keenly against the sky," he comes up with Fancy. We can track them step by step as they proceed towards the school-house.

A little later in the narrative we see the vicar going towards *Casterbridge* – already stated to be an approximation to Dorchester; he falls in with Dick and walks beside him until they reach Grey's Bridge. Dick leaves him to go to *Durnover Mill* (Fordington Mill); but "Mr. Maybold leant over the parapet of the bridge and looked into the river." He had just heard from Dick of his engagement to Fancy, and his heart was heavy. This bridge has often served our author as the supposed resting-place of those whose minds were perturbed – Michael Henchard, in "The Mayor of Casterbridge," and other familiar characters.

We have already discovered the cottage in *Yalbury Wood*, and we turn thither again for the final scene. It is the day of the wedding, and many old friends are gathered there. We see them starting for the church – "every man to his maid. . . . Now among dark perpendicular firs . . . now through a hazel copse . . . now under broad beeches in bright young leaves they threaded their way into the high road over *Yalbury Hill*, which dipped at the point directly into the village of Fancy's parish". No name is given, but we may take it for granted that the reference is to *Weatherbury* – pictured from the Puddletown of long ago – which we have visited in a previous chapter.

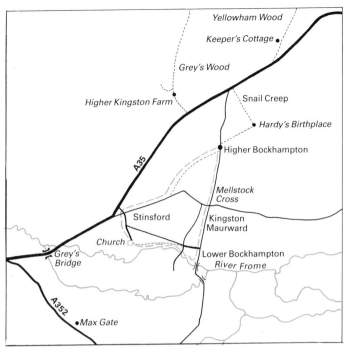

In the Footsteps of the Mellstock Choir

Stinsford Church *(Mellstock Church)*
William Dewy, Tranter Reuben, Farmer Ledlow late at plough,
      Robert's kin, and John's, and Ned's,
And the Squire, and Lady Susan, lie in Mellstock Churchyard now!

Friends Beyond

Here the little church of Stinsford comes before us, though of course in the old guise in which we see it at the time of "Under the Greenwood Tree".

The Mother Mourns

In the western portion of *Egdon Heath* the highest horizon line is backed by the dense trees of Yellowham Woods. Deep dark recesses are to be found in these woods, spots where the sunlight rarely enters in summer because of the thick leaf-curtains, where squirrels leap from branch to branch and the shy woodpecker finds a home. Here is the setting for the present poem, in the *Yalbury Woods*, already familiar to us as forming one of the backgrounds in "Under the Greenwood Tree."

I Need Not Go

There is nothing for us to remark here except the prime fact that Stinsford Churchyard holds the tomb in which *She* lies.

Long Plighted

Again the country of Yellowham Woods comes before us, with its surrounding of *Egdon Heath*.

The Voice of the Thorn

Doubtless this poem might have been suggested by any thorn on any down, but familiarity with our author's methods leads us to suppose that a particular thorn tree was before him as he wrote. This was in fact the case. From Upper Bockhampton there is a footpath leading across Kingston Park to Stinsford Church, and here we can see old thorn trees, many of which strike us as reasonably typical.

A Church Romance

The church of Stinsford would seem to serve for the background of this sonnet-scene, but before the West Gallery and high pews were removed. It will be remembered that the music here was performed by a string choir – just as we read of it in "Under the Greenwood Tree."

The Christening

As we explore the old church of Puddletown we cannot help noticing the worn "gallery stairs." Until about the year 1840 the music, here as at Stinsford, was produced by a string choir. In "the woods afar" we let our thoughts turn to Yellowham Woods, another feature in the book just mentioned.

The Dead Quire

This takes us again into the *Mellstock* country and to the church of Stinsford. The "dormered inn" is no longer the licensed house of former years, but we may trace its likeness in the thatch-roofed dwelling close to the bridge at Lower Bockhampton. Passing through the "Bank-walk wicket," a pathway leads us beside the margin of the "crystal Froom"; we leave it to mount the rise called "Church-way" ("Church Lane" elsewhere), and after passing the church we continue an upward path, called here "Moaning Hill" by our author, the name coming doubtless from the weird sound made by the wind as it passes among the twigs and branches of the clump of chestnut trees just in front. The "Mead of Memories" is, of course, represented by the watered ground below the church.

The Noble Lady's Tale

Stinsford again forms a background, and in the church we come upon the "yellowing marble" with the pair of linked hearts, which forms the Monument spoken of in the poem.

Yell'ham Wood's Story

"Coom-Firtrees" stand on a slight eminence just outside the Coomb – a grassy eweleaze close to Puddletown and on the margin of *Egdon Heath*. "Clyffe-hill Clump" is a high, wind-swept, fir-crowned hill standing on the ridge which separates the valleys of the Froom and Pydel, and recognisable as a familiar landmark from long distances. Just below is the little hamlet of Clyffe. "Yell'ham Wood" scarcely needs further elucidation, for it has already come before us frequently in our explorations.

THE
COUNTRY
OF
"WESSEX TALES"

The Three Strangers

This very popular story, both in narrative and as a play, has for its scenery a locality which seems particularly appropriate. If we journey to Grimstone and take our way up Long Ash Lane, the old Roman Road which led from Dorchester to Yeovil, we shall note on our right hand a wind-swept, desolate country which seems to echo the voices we hear in imagination coming from the cottage standing on "the solitary hill of Higher Crowstairs." It is all very forlorn, very sombre; strangers are rarely seen here, and only those frequent the downs whose work lies thereon. From the top of the downs a wide view of the surrounding country can be had. To the south-east lies Dorchester, hedged in by its avenues of trees; behind it Bincombe Down and the Ridgeway shut out the sea.

It is to the lonely habitation here that the three strangers are imagined to come. The first to arrive is the escaped prisoner from *Casterbridge* Gaol; the second is the hangman, passing on his way to the very place the other had come from; the third had tramped from *Shottsford*, a town symbolical of Blandford. We may readily picture the hurried exit of the third stranger and his subsequent pursuit by the rest of the party, armed with lanterns and hurdle-staves; and in imagination we watch them scrambling over the downs, falling down the lynchets, and eventually returning with the innocent man in custody.

A Tradition of 1804

Solomon Selby's tale of the "Corsican Tyrant" takes us to Lulworth Cove and the downs that surround it, for we have already pictured Lulworth as approximately identical with *Lulstead* or *Lulwind*. "Uncle Job" is supposed to have been in camp "on the downs above King George's watering-place" – evidently Bincombe Down – and he comes to visit Solomon's father, and goes with the lad at night to look to the sheep. The cottage where Solomon lived is no longer discoverable, and our greed for topographical accuracy must be satisfied with an amble on the downs above Lulworth Cove and a glance down into the Cove itself. To the geologist the cliffs here will prove particularly attractive on account of the different strata to

Higher Crowstairs
Lea indicates the general area of
Higher Crowstairs but is not over
– precise about the building.
However, his archives contain his
original photographs bearing the
caption *The Three Strangers*. One
of these, published now for the
first time, may allow the
topographical puzzle to be solved.

Bincombe Village
Behind the village rises Bincombe
Down (*Overcombe Down*) which
affords spectacular views of the
coastlands.

be observed; while the undulating downs, covered with numerous barrows and some prehistoric earthworks, will delight all who are interested in archaeology.

The Melancholy Hussar of the German Legion

This story is laid on a basis of historical fact, and we can afford to be definite in our identification of the backgrounds. Bincombe Down, soon to be familiar to us as a frequent scene in "The Trumpet-Major," and again to come before us when we explore the country connected with "The Dynasts," is the spot we are seeking. "Here stretch the downs, high and breezy and green, absolutely unchanged since those eventful days," says our author. The down overlooks one of the most extensive panoramas in the whole of the Wessex Country – "commanding the Isle of Portland in front, and reaching to St. Aldhelm's Head eastward and almost to the Start on the West."

The association of ancient days, of people who have long ago passed into dust, seems to linger around this grassy expanse, and we should find it difficult to conjure up a more fitting scene for the enactment of the tragedy which forms the *motif* of the story.

"The small, dilapidated, half farm half manor-house," in which Phyllis Grove is supposed to have lived, has now completely disappeared, leaving no tangible evidence of its existence. Only the church remains as an uninscribed monument to the two comrades. Their bodies lie in the graveyard attached, and the actual spot used to be pointed out by some of the older inhabitants; but there is no memorial tablet, and we must rely on the memory of those who have had the mounds indicated to them by their parents. In the parish register may still be seen the entries relating to the burial of the two deserters, under the date of June 30th, 1801. Men who saw them shot were known to living persons.

The plan of escape formulated by the Hussars seemed simple and promising for success. Phyllis was to meet her lover "at a point in the highway at which the lane to the village branched off," and, as we descend the Ridgeway Hill, we note a steep declivity on our left hand passing under the trees that edge the road and rising again to cross an open field. We recognise the spot at a glance. But for the miscarriage of their plans the lovers would then have made their way into Weymouth, would have crossed the harbour-bridge, climbed over the Nothe, and joined Christoph in the boat.

The Withered Arm

We will take *Holmstoke* to be an approximate representa-

**The Ruins of the Old Church,
Stoke** *(Holmstoke Church)*
Hardy's ruins of *Holmstoke
Church* are still to be seen today.

Holme Farm *("the white house
of ample dimensions")*
Lea identifies Holme Farm at
West Holme as the inspiration for
"the white house". Denys Kay-
Robinson has suggested
Hethfelton House between
Bovington and Stokeford. It is
interesting to see that Lea speaks
of *Holmstoke* as being an
"*approximate* representation" of
East Stoke.

tion of East Stoke, a village on the Frome, three and a half miles west of Wareham. It is on the road from this place – the *Anglebury* of our author's imagining – that we see the farmer driving his wife home to "the white house of ample dimensions . . . with farm buildings and ricks at the back," the prototype of which is still to be found in the adjoining hamlet of West Holme.

The church mentioned in the story was drawn from the ruined aisles which are to be seen in the meadows at the back of the mill. Even at the period to which the story belongs it was spoken of as "an ancient little pile"; but in 1828 the new church was built – now on the other side of the railway constructed later, and close to the high road – since when only occasional services have been held in the decayed ruins.

The cottage which was supposed to shelter Rhoda Brook stood at "a lonely spot high above the watermeads and not far from the border of Egdon Heath." It has no particular description given to distinguish it from other similar cottages in the vicinty, but in any case we may assume that it has perished long ago. We may well conjecture where it stood, probably to the southward of the hamlet.

The story brings before us vividly one of the old-time superstitions which are now fast dying out. The dream which came to Rhoda is an incident by no means uncommon, and similar occurrences have been repeatedly brought before the writer of this Guide. By a certain class of people it would perhaps be referred to as a nightmare; amongst the less literate such a dreamer would describe herself as being "hag-rod," *i.e.* hag-ridden. Numberless cases could be quoted where such visitations have occurred, sometimes by day, but generally by night; and doubtless the recorded instances would be much more common, were it not that the sufferers are chary of mentioning the facts, save to those who will be more likely to show sympathy than scepticism.

The house in which Conjuror Trendle was supposed to live has fallen into complete decay; the walls were still standing twenty years ago, but we can only find the foundations now, and these are half hidden under a tangle of heather and brambles. Passing the spot some years ago, the writer inquired of an old rustic who was working near whether he remembered it when it was occupied, and he replied that a man used to live there who was "a seventh of a seventh," meaning a seventh son of a seventh son – a qualification considered as. a strict essential for the holding of occult powers. These "conjurors," or (of the other sex) "cunning women," or "white witches" – as they were variously styled – once formed an important section

The Hangman's Cottage, Dorchester *(Casterbridge)*
The cottage was home for the hangman in Hardy's day, but the outside flight of stairs noticed by Gertrude Lodge is no longer to be seen. Hardy witnessed two hangings when he was a boy. (Executions were regularly held in public until 1867 in England.)

Clyffe Clump
A familiar landmark for many miles, Clyffe Clump is a high mound, capped with firs, which divides the valleys of the Frome and the Pydel.

of rural communities, but they are seldom heard of now.

We may picture Mrs. Lodge and Rhoda as they "set out on their climb into the interior of this solemn country," passing along the old highway which follows the ridge separating the two valleys of the Froom and the Pydel, and known as the Puddletown to Wareham Road. We have passed along it before in imagination when Diggory Venn came to Rainbarrow with his van and the shaggy heath-croppers. From the ridge extends a magnificent view on both hands, and many objects of interest to Hardy readers may be noted. Straight before us is Clyffe Clump, standing this side of the little village of *Stickleford*, with Rainbarrow behind it. On our right hand, in the Pydel Vale, lie the villages *Kingsbere* and *East Egdon*, the former backed by *Greenhill* – scene of the fair in "Far from the the Madding Crowd." On the left hand, in the Valley of the Froom, lies *Holmstoke*, also *Wellbridge*, and in the distance forming the horizon are the hills that shut in *Lulstead Cove* and the country which forms the landscapes in "The Distracted Preacher."

It is understood to be about six years later that Gertrude visits the Conjuror for the second time, and it is then that she learns how a cure may be brought about. In consequence of this we see her riding towards *Casterbridge* in order to reach the gaol. "She did not take the direct road thither through *Stickleford* (relatively Tincleton)," but rode by a roundabout course until she entered the heath. When she at length reaches *Casterbridge* it is almost dark. At the entrance to the town stands that old hostelry the White Hart, a portion of which building overhangs the Froom, and here she stables her horse. We see her treading the path that runs beside the river – a path we have already traversed in the footsteps of Henchard – passing the old Priory Mill, and at length reaching the little thatched cottage which was her destination. It is called the Hangman's Cottage to this day. On the end wall may be traced the opening which formed the doorway to the upper room, which was reached by an outside flight of stairs.

On the following day we see her in our mind's eye undergoing the gruesome process known as "turning the blood," once credited by many people as an infallible cure for certain obscure diseases which defied medical diagnosis and treatment, and still believed in by some of the older generation of Wessex folk. We hear of Lodge returning home for a time, and then going to *Port Bredy* – a town we shall presently recognise as being drawn after the pattern of Bridport – where he ends his days.

Bridport *(Port Bredy)*
The town hall and (Black) Bull
Hotel can still be visited today.

Lucy Savile's Home
Due to modern building it is no
longer possible to espie Lucy
Savile's home in the manner
suggested by Lea.

Fellow Townsmen

The surroundings and scenery which figure in this story are to be found in and about the old-world town of Bridport, just alluded to in the previous story. *Port Bredy* bears the imprint of having once been a much larger and more important place; a ramble through the streets suggests at a glance that it has had a past history attaching to it of which its present guise gives but scant indication. This conjecture we find to be a true one; there is still a certain amount of commerce carried on within its boundaries, but only on a scale which is a mere echo of its former commercial importance.

It is recorded in Domesday Book that Bridport possessed a mint and an ecclesiastical establishment. Ropes, twines, fishing-nets, and the like, are still manufactured to some extent, but when Henry VIII. was king it was prescribed by royal edict that all the cordage used in the royal navy should be of Bridport manufacture, its renown for ropes and cables dating back to the early part of the thirteenth century. It is interesting to note further that nearly all the flax used for the purpose was grown in the vicinity. Another production for which the town was famous was that of hangmen's ropes; and out of this, which was virtually a monopoly, arose the old saying that So-and-so had been "stabbed with a Bridport dagger" – a polite way of intimating that he had been hanged! The town gets its name from the river Brid or Brit which runs beside it and joins the Asker to flow into the harbour at West Bay.

Let us regard Barnet and Downe as they are imagined driving into the town – "past the little town-hall, the Black Bull Hotel, and onward." We can see the town-hall and the Bull Hotel which served as models; the house in which Downe was supposed to live was probably one of those still visible in the off-street on the right, called Downe Street. The house where Barnet resided has completely disappeared; the site on which it stood, nearly opposite St. Mary's Church, is now occupied by a chapel.

The town-hall was erected in 1786, and stands on the site of the ancient Chapel of St. Andrew. The Bull Hotel is a much older building; it was demised by Daniel Taylor in the time of Charles II. to pay for a schoolmaster to instruct the children of the town. *Château Ringdale* may have been studied from a house just out of the town on the western side encircled in trees, but for the purposes of the story we must imagine it placed near the road that leads to the harbour, now West Bay.

St. Mary's Church was where Lucy Savile was supposed to be married to Downe. There are some interesting

Melbury Osmond *(King's Hintock)*
"It was one of those sequested spots outside the gates of the world where may usually be found more meditation than action, and more listlessness than meditation . . ."

The White Horse Hotel, Maiden Newton *(The White Horse Inn, Chalk-Newton)*
The original Tudor hostelry was pulled down in the late nineteenth century.

monuments in this building, and a climb to the top of the tower will reward us with fine view of the surrounding country.

If we now walk along the Harbour Road we shall pass the supposed site of *Château Ringdale*; and just before we reach West Bay we may note on the right-hand side, standing a little back from the highway, a cottage which from its position seems to suggest the little house where Lucy lived. Continuing, we soon reach West Bay, the seaside suburb of Bridport, and see before us the "little haven, seemingly a beginning made by Nature herself of a perfect harbour."

Interlopers at the Knap

Long Ash Lane is still "a monotonous track without a village or hamlet for many miles, and with very seldom a turning." This is the old Roman Road which leads from Dorchester to Yeovil and is now seldom used, travellers preferring the lower and easier road which passes through Maiden Newton. Following the ancient highway, as did the three equestrians in the story, we shall in due course reach the forking roads at which they halted, a place we recognise as Holywell. We are informed that had they taken the left-hand road they would have come upon "an old house with mullioned windows of Ham-hill stone, and chimneys of lavish solidity. It stood at the top of a slope beside King's Hintock village street. . . ." *King's Hintock* is approximately Melbury Osmund, but the house, still remembered, has been demolished. Inside this house we await the arrival of Phillip and his wife. They had travelled through *Evershead* (Evershot), we are told, and he had looked in at the *Sow-and-Acorn*, an inn we perceive to be the "Acorn."

In this story is mentioned the curious custom of "telling the bees" after a death – a superstition still believed in by most of the inhabitants of rural Wessex; the efficacy is supposed to be guaranteed if supplemented by the affixing of a small piece of crape to each hive. A case came before the writer of these pages a few years ago where the survivors omitted to take this precaution, with the result that the bees, numbering fifty or more stocks, all died. Similar cases can be vouched for where the thing has happened.

The *White Horse* Inn at *Chalk-Newton* formed the half-way house between Darton's Farm and *King's Hintock* and here Helena's boy is handed over to the care of Darton's bailiff. *Chalk-Newton* is more or less synonymous with Maiden Newton, and in the main street of this little town we find the inn mentioned. It was a fine old

Owermoigne Village *(Nether Moynton)*
The scene of "The Distracted Preacher".

Owermoigne Church *(Nether Moynton Church)*
Here Lizzie Newberry guided Stockdale in the dark on the first night of his arrival in order that he should have a warming draught for his cold. It survives as Lea describes it here, the tower in which the smugglers lay concealed remaining intact since the rebuilding in 1883.

Elizabethan specimen of a hostelry, but was pulled down about twenty years ago. There is no clue given us by which we can discover the actual position of Darton's residence, but as it was twenty miles from *King's Hintock* we may safely conclude it lay at no great distance from Dorchester.

The Distracted Preacher

It is the little village of Owermoigne, lying just off the road from Weymouth or Dorchester to Wareham, which is used under the assumed name of *Nether Moynton* as the background for this story. It was once the home of many a smuggler, and some of the old people living there now can remember taking part in smuggling enterprises; but the reticence which in those days was essential to successful undertakings of this kind still lingers, and they prefer to clothe their reminiscences in the guise of "what father did say," or "what granfer twold I" – an allusion which we may safely conclude to be a veil – and only when they get thoroughly warmed up to their recitals does the impersonal note merge into the personal.

The village is only a short three miles from the coast, and is close to that portion of it which is shut in by high, unscalable cliffs, with sparsely populated downlands intervening. Thus we see how well situated it was as a home for such as delighted in defrauding the revenue – some by reason of the profits to be made, others from the love of excitement and adventure. Such episodes as the one described in our story were by no means uncommon in "the good old days," and many ingenious hiding-places are still in existence.

The Church of Owermoigne is a building in the Gothic style, but was rebuilt in 1883 – a date subsequent to the story. Accordingly, we no longer find the "singing gallery stairs" where, under a pile of church debris, "decayed framework, pews, panels, and pieces of flooring," the barrels of illicit spirits were stored.

The house in which Lizzie Newberry was imagined to have lived was drawn from the house which stands almost opposite to the rectory; but the orchard belonging to her cousin Owlett does not quite adjoin her garden. It can, however, still be seen a little way off, and the remains of the artificial cave are perceptible as an irregularity in the ground.

Let us follow in the footsteps of Lizzie when she goes to the cliffs at night to take her part in the landing of the cargo. Leaving Owermoigne, we cross the high road and ascend the steep hill leading towards *Ringsworth* (Ringstead). At its summit we obtain a fine bird's-eye view of

Warmwell Cross *(Warm'ell
Cross)*
The scene of the ambushing of
the excisemen in *The Distracted
Preacher*; they were bound to a
tree and left to shout for help.

the country to the north, east, and west. Then we descend on the other side, and soon pass "the lonely hamlet of Holworth (figuring under its own name)," and soon after are in sight and sound of the sea.

We can imagine them crossing Chaldon Down, meeting the other members of the gang, and continuing till they reach "the crest of the hill at a lonely, trackless place not far from the ancient earthwork called Round Pond." If we glance at the ordnance map we shall be able to dog their footsteps over the undulating downs, crowned here and there with prehistoric barrows, and amid a wealth of scenery of exceeding diversity.

Nether Moynton is again the arena when the excisemen make their raid and at length discover the hiding-places of the smugglers, and then the action changes to *Warm'ell Cross* (Warmwell Cross) – the point where the roads to Weymouth and Dorchester part. Here we see clumps of trees, and it does not require a very vivid imagination to picture the scene described, and to see in fancy the disappointed excisemen bound to the trees and shouting for help, a performance said to have been really enacted in the eighteen-thirties.

THE
COUNTRY
OF

"THE TRUMPET-MAJOR"

The plot of this romance rests on the anticipated landing of Napoleon in England, and is based – we are told in the preface – on facts that were handed down to posterity by local individuals who were themselves actively interested. The shadow cast by Napoleon on the southern coast of Wessex was of sufficient density to make the fact of his landing appear strangely probable. If to the actual evidence of his intended visit we add the influence of naturally superstitious temperaments, we need not be surprised to hear of the consequent precautions taken by the inhabitants of the towns and villages near the coast to guard against being caught unawares; of the systematic training of the local men; or the storage of weapons and ammunition in churches and similar safe retreats. Nor can we doubt that the elaborate arrangements made by many of the better-class people, to fly inland directly the news of his accomplished landing was flashed abroad by the beacon fires prepared on the hills, were the result of actual fear.

The country which forms the groundwork for the chief scenes lies in and around *Budmouth* – a place which we shall regard as being typical of Weymouth. If we accept *Overcombe* as representing Sutton Poyntz, a village lying just under Bincombe Down, it must not be in too narrow a sense, restricted by the actual confines of that village, since it embraces certain features of Upwey, and perhaps Bincombe too.

The action commences here, at *Overcombe* – that is to say, as far as the local situation is concerned. The mill is drawn, not from the mill which once stood in the village of Sutton Poyntz, but from the one it probably resembled – that at Upwey, which we may see still exhibiting many of the features described in the book. Let us, then, imagine the Upwey mill to be standing in the village of Sutton Poyntz, where we also find the "large, smooth mill-pond" of our author's imagining, in which the cavalry watered their horses, and which was in full view of Ann Garland's window.

"On the other side of the mill-pond was an open cross," we read; it is quickly revealed to us as we stand beside the mill-pond. "Behind this a steep slope rose high into the

Sutton Poyntz *(Overcombe)*
Overcombe of the novel is
equated by Lea with Sutton
Poyntz (off the A353 at the
southern base of White Horse hill)
and should not be confused with
Overcombe, south of Preston.

Upwey Mill *(Overcombe Mill)*
Not only does the mill possess
features described in the book,
but it is still in full working order.

sky, merging in a wide and open down." This description
we likewise easily verify. We shall examine the down
again when the scenery of "The Dynasts" comes before us.
It is one of those features occurring in the Wessex Novels
and Poems which remains precisely the same, year in and
year out; it has been very little tampered with, and looks
the same to-day as it did when the White Horse was being
cut out by the encamping soldiery and the sweeping
undulations were dotted with gorgeous uniforms and
white canvas.

Our interest is quickly aroused in this down, and in
fancy we watch the pitching of the tents and the various
other arrangements consequent on the arrival of the
soldiers, including the work of "making a zig-zag path
down the incline from the camp to the riverhead." This
track may still be discerned and followed. When the novel
appeared an old gentleman of ninety wrote to inform the
author that he witnessed the arrival, which was exactly as
described.

We may make up our minds to recognise Poxwell Hall as
the prototype of the *Oxwell Hall* of the story, the home of
Squire Derriman. Its "grey, weatherworn front" is familiar
to every traveller passing it on the Weymouth-Wareham
road. The fine old gate-house lends it an intensified
interest, although this has been altered considerably from
what it was pictured in the story.

Warmwell seems by its position to suggest *Springham* –
the village whither Ann journeyed to the christening
party.

Budmouth itself often claims our attention. It was when
the king was on his way thither that the *Overcombe* folk
climbed to the top of Ridgeway to see him pass. He was to
change horses at "Woodyates Inn" – a hostel near
Cranborne which still bears traces of its former importance as a posting-house. The miller and his party waited at
the summit of the hill until after "the bell of St. Peter's,
Casterbridge – in E flat" – a fine note, still to be heard –
had chimed three o'clock, when the long-expected cortege
at length came in sight on "the white line of road". We can
well imagine the enthusiasm which filled the hearts of the
villagers as they shouted "Long life to King Jarge." These
were stirring times, and excitement ran high when the
routine of daily life was broken in upon by the sudden
advent of the soldiers on the down. People frequently
went to visit the encampment, and we see the miller
taking his friends there on a Sunday evening.

When the review was held, "the whole population of
Overcombe . . . ascended the slope with the crowds from
afar," and if we follow them in imagination we may hear

The Ridgeway
The summit marks the spot
where the Overcombe folk waited
all night to see the King arrive.

Weymouth Harbour (Budmouth)
Weymouth lies on the coast due
south of Dorchester on the A354.
Note the "houses of the
merchants, some ancient
structures of solid stone . . ."

The White Horse
Cut in the hillside in 1808. "We
may now, if we choose, climb the
hill-side and act precisely as Ann
Garland did on her visit there with
the Trumpet Major, namely pace
'from the horse's head down his
breast to his hoof, back by way of
the king's bridle-arm, past the
bridge of his nose, and into his
cocked hat,' or, if we prefer it, we
may follow the Trumpet Major's
example, and stand 'in a
melancholy attitude within the
rowel of his majesty's right
spur.'" (Lea)

The Old Greyhound Inn
The 16th-century arched stone
doorway is all that remains of the
old inn in South Street,
Dorchester.

the exclamations which burst from the lips of the onlook-
ers. It was while witnessing these excitements that Miller
Loveday was apprised of the fact that a letter waited for
him at the *Budmouth* post office; and it drew from him the
remark that "there *was* a letter in the candle". This
interesting superstition has almost died out, disappearing
concurrently with the "tallow dip," but it still persists here
and there in "outstep placen." The letter heralds the
coming of Bob Loveday, and soon after his arrival we read
of him journeying to *Casterbridge* (Dorchester) to meet his
fiancée. The "Old Greyhound Inn," where he puts up his
horse, is still to be found in South Street, but has long lost
its licence. We see him standing at the Bow watching the
road in the direction of Grey's Bridge, until he sees the
coach from *Melchester* – the city we have come to look at as
closely resembling Salisbury – where his lady-love had
been staying with her aunt. But as she does not arrive, he
beguiles the hours by "wandering up and down the
pavement," evidently somewhere close to the church of
All-Saints, since the voices of worshippers come to him
through the open windows.

The soldiers go into barracks at *Exonbury* – the city we
think of as Exeter. We are recalled to the down by the
kindling of the beacon fire, an incident repeated in "The
Dynasts"; and as we shall examine this later on it need not
detain us now. The alarm had the effect of sending the
women-folk inland, and amongst the refugees we see our
friends from *Overcombe Mill* hastening towards *Kingsbere*
– the townlet we have already recognised as Bere Regis.
The old order for their retreat thither still exists. They were
pursued by Festus Derriman, after he had learned to his
satisfaction and relief that the report of Napoleon's
landing was false. He "cantered on over the hill (Ridgeway), meeting on his route the Lower Longpuddle or
Weatherbury (Puddletown) volunteers." The lonely cottage in which he besieged Ann is still to be seen amid the
farther downs above Holcombe Bottom, but it is now in a
state of complete ruin.

The episode of the press-gang brings before us very
vividly the date at which the incidents were imagined to
have taken place, for impressment died out at the end of
the Napoleonic wars in 1815. We see Ann driving back
from *Budmouth* with her lover; she glances apprehensively
in the direction of the ships lying at anchor in the bay
towards Portland, whose "dark contour, lying like a whale
on the sea," is readily discerned.

We may follow the Trumpet-Major and Ann when they
go to see the White Horse, cut out on the chalky hill-side
by the soldiers. "After pacing from the horse's head down

Poxwell House *(Oxwell Hall)*
Note "the arched gateway which
screened the main front; over it
was the porter's lodge reached by
a spiral staircase." The residence
of "Old Derriman" with its "grey,
weatherworn front" lies off the
Weymouth-Wareham road
(A353).

The Faringdon Ruin
This ruin can be seen from the
A352 (Dorchester-Wareham road)
in a meadow beyond Winterborne
Came. It was here that Ann
Garland tried to talk of marriage.

his breast to his hoof, back by way of the king's bridle-arm, past the bridge of his nose, and into his cocked hat, Ann said that she had had enough of it, and stepped out of the chalk clearing upon the grass. The Trumpet-Major had remained all the time in a melancholy attitude within the rowel of his Majesty's right spur." We may follow either of these actions. The easiest ascent to the White Horse is from Sutton Poyntz; but if we walk along the top of the ridge from Bincombe Down, and turn to the right over the crest of the hill, thus suddenly finding ourselves surrounded by patches of bare, chalky earth, we shall be set wondering as to their meaning, for no resemblance can be traced to the horse or its rider as they appear from the opposite hill, where the road winds up from Preston Village.

Pos'ham, which is the colloquial rendering of Portesham, was the birthplace of Captain Hardy – Nelson's Hardy – one of a collateral branch of the Dorset Hardys – and in the village we can find his house; while the steep hill going northwards out of the village will bring us to the monument which stands solitary on Blagdon, or Blackdown. In the story, Bob visits the Captain in his home, and the result of his interview is that he joins the *Victory* and sails away.

Portland Bill, or Beal, comes before us as a vantage-point when Ann goes there to catch a last glimpse of the ship. We may picture her journey by carrier to *Budmouth*; then, crossing the Fleet in a rowing-boat – for a bridge was lacking at that time, – she climbs the steep road to the top of Portland – "the huge lump of freestone which forms the peninsula" – and in due course reaches "the extreme southerly peak of rock" from which she watches "the great silent ship" as it passes and disappears. We shall visit "the wild, herbless, weather-worn promontory" again, when we search for the scenery figuring in the poem entitled "Souls of the Slain."

After Bob's departure on board the *Victory* we see Ann and John walking side by side until they come to "a gable, known as Faringdon Ruin," under which title it still may be found in Came Park, close to Dorchester, and is all that now remains of the church and the village which once stood there.

This meeting prepares us for the closing incidents of the story. "Uncle Benjy" dies, and *Oxwell Hall*, with its "muddy quadrangle, archways, mullioned windows, cracked battlements, and weed-grown garden," becomes the property of Ann Garland. And from the doors of the familiar mill we catch our last glimpse of John as he "marches into the night."

The Well-Beloved

This poem, it should be noted, has no connection with the novel bearing the same title. Its setting (in the Wessex Edition) is at Jordan Hill, near Weymouth – the ancient Roman station Clavinium – where there are the remains of a Roman temple, tessellated pavements, and other relics of the Roman occupation. *Jordon Grove* speaks to us of Preston Vale, a well-wooded depression hard by. Artistic Roman pottery has been found in large quantities hereabouts, and good examples of Samian ware.

The Lacking Sense

The background here is Waddon Vale, that deep valley running from Upwey towards Abbotsbury. High above it on the northern side is Blagdon, or Blackdown, whence the Hardy Monument rises skywards.

The Alarm

Here we are taken into the atmosphere of, and over some of the ground traversed in, "The Trumpet-Major" and "The Dynasts." The homestead "in a ferny byway" lay not far from Upper Bockhampton, and here we picture the volunteer bidding his wife farewell ere he takes the road for "Royal George's Town" – an obvious description of Weymouth. Before he starts he bids his wife be prepared to journey to *Kingsbere* – the townlet we have seen to be Bere Regis – should rumour reach her of Napoleon's landing. It was, in fact, the spot mentioned in the Government Orders of the date for the retreat of women and children.

This was on the day following the kindling of the beacons, and as he journeys onward he sees "The Barrow-Beacon burning – burning low," on Rainbarrows – an ancient burial-place which bulks largely in "The Return of the Native" and also in "The Dynasts." We will follow in his footsteps. When he reaches the river Froom he hesitates whether to proceed or to turn back; but his mind is made up for him by watching the flight of the bird he releases from the river weeds, which bears over the river, crosses *Durnover Great-Field* (Fordington Field), and continues due southward. Then he pursues his way, passing *Mai-Don*, and climbing Ridgeway Hill. Maiden Castle we shall examine more closely in "After the Club Dance," and the Ridgeway when we are exploring the scenery of "The Dynasts."

THE
COUNTRY
OF
"TWO ON A TOWER"

In the preface to this book we are told that "the scene of action was suggested by two real spots in the part of the country specified, each of which has a column standing upon it. Certain surrounding peculiarities have been imported into the narrative from both sides." The characteristics pertaining to the two spots are easily determined. The actual building is drawn in the main from the tower standing in Charborough Park, a few miles south of Wimborne Minster; while the immediate setting of the fictitious observatory shows us the position occupied by a shaft or obelisk which rises from a hill near Milborne St. Andrew, between Blandford and Dorchester.

We will examine the situation first. To quote from the book: "The central feature of the middle distance . . . was a circular isolated hill . . . covered with fir-trees. . . ." The obelisk is known locally as "Milborne Speer" or "Ring's-Hill Speer" – the latter title being an allusion to the entrenched earthwork from which the spire rises. Some few years ago the trees on the summit of the hill were thinned, and to-day the spire stands out boldly before the eyes of the traveller on the Dorchester-Blandford road. The monument bears the date of 1761; it is built chiefly of brick, with stone quoins; the initials "E. M. P." stand for Edmund Morton Pleydell, in whose memory it was erected.

The origin of the earthwork is open to question – a fact to which our author draws attention. "The fir-shrouded hill-top was (according to some antiquaries) an old Roman camp, – if it were not (as others insisted) an old British castle, or (as the rest swore) an old Saxon field of Witenagemote, – with remains of an outer and inner vallum." If we visit the spot in spring we shall be struck at once with the natural wild-flower garden which surrounds the spire. Bluebells, cowslips, campions in many shades of red and pink, whitethorn, and the mealy guelder-rose literally cover the ground. As though to impress us with its isolated position, we may see hovering over the spot the kestrels which nest there almost every year, and have done from time immemorial. The original trenches are almost level with the banks, for the fir-needles have dropped into them year after year, and the

The Two Towers

Hardy modelled his fictional tower on the architecture of Charborough tower but located it at the site of Ring's-Hill Speer (near Milborne St Andrew). On the back of the original photograph Hardy himself remarks: "The tower being so important in the story there should be two [Hardy's underlining] pictures of it – one of each of the combined towers (vide preface)." On another photograph, Hardy makes it clear that too much emphasis on Charborough Park itself would give the erroneous impression that this was its fictional setting rather than a hill near Milborne St Andrew where the obelisk [right] resides.

A Tale of Two Towers

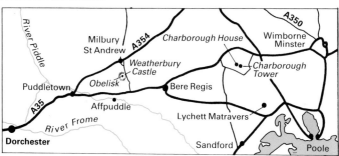

Charborough House *(Welland House)*

footfalls of a visitor are muffled as though he trod a pile carpet. The earthwork is known as Weatherbury Castle, and hints to us whence came our author's fictitious name for Puddletown.

The tower in Charborough Park – more particularly the column of the novel – is 120 feet in height, and from the summit extends a magnificent view of the surrounding country. It is a conspicuous land-mark, visible from a distance of many miles and from several different directions. It is described in the book as having been built "in the Tuscan order of classic architecture," which is literally correct.

A flight of wide, moss-grown steps leads up to the tower; the exterior is decorated with some interesting grotesques. Just inside is a tablet which tells us the tower was erected in 1790, was struck by lightning in 1838, and was considerably damaged. In the year following it was rebuilt, forty feet being added. A heavy moulded handrail guides us to the top, where we enter a room panelled in chestnut and fitted with some handsomely carved seats, from whence the view is seen through the many windows. We recognise the Hardy Monument on Blackdown; the long range of the Purbeck Hills; Bournemouth, backed by the New Forest; Studland; and a portion of the Channel. With a pair of glasses we should make out many familiar landmarks.

Close to this tower is Charborough House, the prototype of the *Welland House* of the story. It stands in a finely timbered park, wherein is a magnificent herd of deer, also some cattle of Asiatic breed. In the grounds is an interesting grotto, the front surmounted by a figure of Fame, and bearing an inscription recording the fact that the plan of the Great Revolution was formulated therein in the year 1686. Near the house is the church; this and the adjacent graveyard form the backgrounds for some short scenes.

Wimborne Minster, in its fictitious presentment of *Warborne*, interests us as being the place where St. Cleeve was supposed to be educated. According to Haymoss, it was "a place where they draw up young gam'sters' brains like rhubarb under a ninepenny pan." The first college was founded here in 1043 by Edward the Confessor, and remained unaltered until 1496, when Margaret of Richmond founded a chantry and established a school connection with it. The old Grammar School buildings were demolished and new ones erected in 1851. Wimborne is an ancient town, thought by some to be identical with the Vindogladia of the Antonine Itinerary. The fine church or minster forms the most notable feature, the central part

The Roman Baths at Bath
"And the people of Bath . . . never need to light their fires except as a luxury, for the water springs up out of the earth ready boiled for use." Bath enjoyed popularity as a spa in the 18th and 19th centuries. It then became famous for its antiquarian remains.

Wimborne Minster *(Warborne)*
Swithin St Cleeve was educated at the school in *Warborne*. This town was for a while the home of Thomas Hardy and his first wife Emma, and the place where Hardy wrote *Two on a Tower*. The graveyard of the Minster, levelled of its tombstones by "zealous Churchmen's pick and plane" became the subject of his poetical attack "The Levelled Churchyard".

dating from the twelfth century; it contains many interesting monuments, including a brass bearing the date of 873, supposed to mark the resting-place of King Aethelred. Under the west tower is an orrery clock, which is said to have been going since the fourteenth century, and which was made by Peter Lightfoot, a monk of Glastonbury. In the chapel of Holy Trinity is a Saxon chest 1100 years old. In a room above the vestry is the famous chained library, founded in the sixteenth century.

Little Welland Village would seem to be more or less a counterpart of Winterborne Zelstone; its importance in the action of the narrative is not great. The "venerable thatched house . . . built of chalk in the lump," in which St. Cleeve was imagined to have lived, cannot now be found, and has probably perished since the time of the story.

The city of Bath figures under its own name and forms one of the backgrounds. Here we can picture Lady Constantine "wandering about beneath the aisles" of the Abbey. Bath, that place of steep, abrupt hills, terraced to accommodate the roads and houses rising in tiers above the valley of the Avon, with its two distinct legends ascribing the foundation of the city to a British king, Bladud, is too well known to need description. The mineral springs from which it takes its name were long used by the Romans, and the Baths are justly considered to represent one of the finest Roman antiquities in Western Europe.

Greenwich Observatory, Southampton Docks, and The Cape figure in this novel to some extent; then for a time the action takes us to *Melchester*, which is tantamount to Salisbury. Here we read of the "precincts of the damp and venerable Close," and are presently introduced to the "episcopal palace," depicted doubtless from the picturesque irregular building which is still the residence of the bishop.

The Levelled Churchyard

Although this poem might with justice refer to many of our churchyards, the particular one in our author's mind was evidently that of Wimborne, where ducks and drakes were played with the headstones at the "Restoration" to a truly amazing extent.

THE
COUNTRY
OF
"THE WELL-BELOVED"

(A Sketch of a Temperament)

It is to Portland, "the Peninsula carved by Time out of a single stone," that we must go to find the surroundings which served for this romance – or satire. Nearly all the action takes place here, on this mysterious storm-lashed eminence, known to us in the Wessex Novels and Poems as "The Isle of Slingers," "The Isle by the Race," and other titles similarly descriptive of Portland. Commonly designated an island, it is in reality a peninsula, connected with the mainland by a thin neck of pebbles called the Chesil Beach, or Bank – chesil being derived from an Anglo-Saxon word meaning pebble. The Bank varies in width, but is at no point wider than two hundred yards. The gales which sweep over it from the south-west are phenomenal in force, coming straight off the Atlantic, and the waves in the West Bay, or Deadman's Bay, are literally mountains high. The present writer has driven along the road in a dog-cart more than once when the vehicle has been swung half round by the force of the wind. Deadman's Bay is well named, for if a vessel once gets inside it during a gale, there is only the remotest possibility of its ever getting out again, and a practical certainty of its being dashed to pieces on the beach.

The Island – to call it by its colloquial name – has an atmosphere splendidly curative of chest diseases, as shown by its effect on soldiers quartered there. The cliffs are precipitous, and only a few spots on the southern side are accessible from the sea. Although subdivided into several villages, to the Islanders themselves there seem to be two main distinctive divisions – "Top o' Hill" and "Under Hill." Its ancient history is difficult to discover with any great exactness. Saxon, Roman, and Dane all had their day without doubt, but very few records remain to testify to the length of their occupation. The old-time barrows, the earthworks, the stone circles, all of which were represented half a century ago, have been destroyed by quarry extensions and building operations. Portland is connected in most people's minds with the convict establishment – that fastness from which it is boasted no prisoner has escaped alive; in fact, every visitor who goes to the Island to-day is accosted by numerous would-be

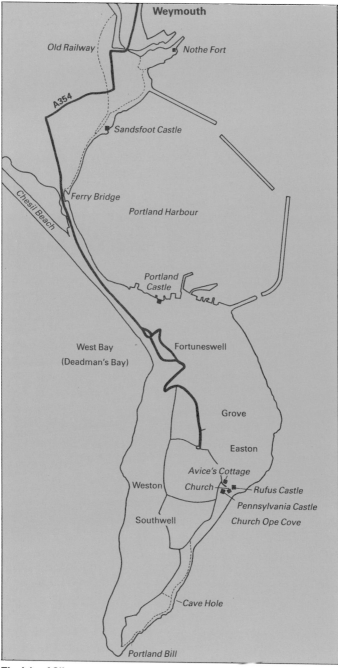

The Isle of Slingers

guides, eager to take him to spots from which the convicts may be seen at work. For those who are of sufficiently morbid turn of mind it is possible, or used to be quite recently, to obtain for the modest sum of sixpence a tea which includes a window-sight of the prison yard! The majority of us will probably be satisfied with a ramble over the Island and a look at some of the quarries which have become world famous. The oölitic limestone obtained here has been used for many important buildings in the country, including St. Paul's Cathedral.

We are told in the preface that this is the "home of a curious and well-nigh distinct people, cherishing strange beliefs and singular customs now for the most part obsolescent." It is with regret that we notice the extermination of these idiosyncrasies, for Portland has altered out of all recognition during the last few generations. Naturally, any sort of insulation tends to keep back progress of the race, particularly as regards mental development, and until recent years the Islanders were a long way behind the dwellers on the mainland in point of intellectual advancement; and whilst we may, from one standpoint, decry this backwardness, we cannot but appreciate a fact which enabled us to retrace a page in the history of human evolution and gaze on a past link in the chain of life. Similarly, we view the immutable rock which, formed countless centuries ago, has resisted Time's onslaughts till now, and gives itself up grudgingly to the scientifically designed tools and engines in the hands of the quarriers.

With an upward intellectual trend has also occurred a deterioration of physique, accompanied by a more lax moral standard. A point of strange interest to the anthropologist was the fact that, although intermarriage between near relatives was common, yet the mental and physical characteristics of the people displayed no ill effects therefrom. The custom of close-marriage in the Island was due partly to necessity – owing to the isolation and difficulty of communion with neighbouring people – and partly to an unwritten code whereby the people sought to keep themselves distinct. Even nowadays the names are limited in number – a feature which comes before us in the case of many islands and districts naturally isolated. The innate pride of the Portlander still makes him keenly conscious of the distinction between those born on the Island and the stranger, or "kimberlin." The present writer was at Portland recently and entered into conversation with a local man, intimating at the outset that he was merely a kimberlin; to which the Islander replied, "Oh well, I'm a thoroughbred 'un." It was said, too, with an air

Portland
"The peninsula, carved by Time out of a single stone." It was from this "wild, herbless, weatherworn promontory" that Ann Garland watched the departure of the *Victory* in *The Trumpet Major.*

Pennsylvania Castle, Portland
(Sylvania Castle, Isle of Slingers)
"A private mansion of comparatively modern date, in whose grounds stood the single plantation of trees of which the isle could boast." This was the abode of Jocelyn Pierston in *The Well Beloved.* Today the castle is operated as a hotel, its entrance no longer as pictured here. The cottage which Lea describes as standing nearby, and as the model of the Caros' home, also survives. It was renovated and given to the town by its sometime owner, Marie Stopes. It is now a museum.

of conscious superiority which was not lost on his listener. Patriotism is another marked characteristic on this rocky island home. It was one day at the Beal that a casual chat with another of the Islanders brought out his love of the homeland. He had been a soldier, had served in the South African and other campaigns, had visited many of the beauty spots of the world; but nowhere had he found any scenery that appealed to him as did the wild storm-lashed rocks of Portland, where he hoped to live out the rest of his life and be gathered to his fathers in the wind-swept churchyard.

Portland always seems as though wrapped in a cloak of sadness, and holds a sombre atmosphere of which it grows impossible to be oblivious. The countless aeons of time through which our world has been built up is very manifest here, for the geological epochs are strongly marked – a fact sufficient in itself to produce a sobering influence on our minds.

We will now follow Pierston in imagination as he comes upon the scene. Through the *Street of Wells* (Fortune's Well) he passes, and, after a stiff climb up the precipitous hill, walks towards the *Eastern Village* – doubtless a designation of Easton. Here we see him pause before the cottage in which the Caros lived. Coming before the closed gates which form the northern entrance to Pennsylvania Castle, we note a lane on our left hand, and at the corner stands the model of Caros' home. "Like the Island it was all of stone, not only in walls but in window frames, roof, chimneys, fence, stile, pigstye and stable, almost door." Many of these descriptive features may be traced to-day, though certain innovations have crept in which have not added to picturesqueness. It stood close to the house of Pierston's father, the two gardens adjoining.

Pierston renews his early acquaintance with Avice, and soon we watch them taking walks about the Island, visiting the Bill or Beal, and "pausing over the treacherous cavern known as Cave Hole". We are led to the Beal frequently in our explorations; we go thither with Ann Garland in "The Trumpet-Major," and again when it forms the background for the poem entitled "The Souls of the Slain." Cave Hole is one of the many caverns which abound on the Island; its actual position is difficult to describe, but may be easily found by inquiry of a local person. Then we may picture Pierston descending the hill to listen to Avice singing at the village hall, and we may follow them on their subsequent return homewards together. We see them in our mind's eye climbing up the steep hill and pausing at the top to gaze over the bay before them, whence "there arose a deep, hollow stroke

Church-Hope, Portland
This is where Pierston wooed the
first Avice. The ruins still stand
today, as do those of Rufus Castle
(otherwise known as Bow-and-
Arrow Castle), shown below.

Rufus Castle *(Red King's Castle)*
This is where the third Avice met
Leverre on the night of her
elopement.

like the single beat of a drum, the intervals being filled with a long drawn rattling, as of bones between huge canine jaws. It came from the vast concave of Deadman's Bay, rising and falling against the pebble dyke." If we wish to appreciate this truly realistic description we must stand on the hill-top when night is falling or after darkness has set in. Then we may absorb to the full the strange weirdness of this rocky island and become as it were impregnated with the atmosphere which clings to it. Then, and then only, can we hope to obtain a true impression of that "sinister bay," or feel the existence of "the human multitude lying below; those who had gone down in vessels of war, East Indiamen, barges, brigs, and ships of the Armada – select people, common and debased. . . ."

The old graveyard of Church-Hope was supposed to be visited. Of the church itself we can see little to-day, but the headstones around it testify that long-perished inhabitants lie here at rest, in a position hard to beat from the point of view of picturesqueness. The whole mass seems to have slipped down the side of the cliff and narrowly escaped being precipitated into the sea below. This is the most interesting portion of the Island to the botanist; the cliffs here are clothed in wild-flowers, rocks jutting out between the patches of blossoms and forming a rock-garden of nature's fashioning which throws all artificial attempts at emulation into the shade. Just below, the sea washes gently on the sandy beach of the little cove; and as though guarding it from peril there stand the remains of the *Red King's Castle* – Rufus Castle, or Bow-and-Arrow Castle, as it is alternatively called – the very name testifying to the period at which it was built.

When Pennsylvania Castle, in the guise of *Sylvania Castle*, comes before us it is the residence of Marcia Bencomb for the time being. This castle is a comparatively modern building, erected by John Penn, grandson of William Penn, once a governor of Portland and the founder of Pennsylvania. To use our author's words: "It is a private mansion of comparatively modern date, in whose grounds stood the single plantation of trees of which the Island could boast. . . ."

We will follow in Pierston's footsteps when he sets out to walk to *Budmouth-Regis* – approximately Weymouth – by way of the Chesil Beach. It was when a gale was blowing and the rain had "assumed the character of a raking fusillade." We see him overtaking Marcia, and we watch them seeking shelter under one of the upturned lerrets. After a time they renew the struggle to reach *Budmouth*, cross the ferry-bridge – now represented by a

Sandsfoot Castle *(Henry the Eighth's Castle above the sands)*
The Tudor ruins — "on the verge of the ragstone cliff" — are barely changed, though much residential development now characterises the place.

Hope Cove, Portland *(Isle of Slingers)*
"The beautiful little bay . . . marks the spot from whence Avice and Leverre are supposed to have escaped in a rowing boat that had neither oars nor sails." [Lea]

more permanent structure – leave the ruined castle of Sandsfoot on their right hand, and finally enter the town, where they sleep the night at a temperance inn near the station. The next morning they journey to London by train; thither we shall not follow them.

An interval of nearly twenty years elapses before we visit Portland again – this time by train – passing close under Sandsfoot Castle, the fort erected by Henry VIII. for the protection of the shipping. A familiar scene comes before our eyes as we catch sight of the "black lerrets" and "the white cubes of oölite"; and then we climb the accustomed hill and pass across the plateau to the ruined Church-Hope, stranded half-way down the cliff-face. Here, at the graveside of Avice, Pierston sees her daughter. Shortly after this encounter, we read of him as the tenant of *Sylvania Castle*, and we picture him on the evening of his arrival inspecting the house, the garden, and then entering the "garden-house of Elizabethan design, which stood on the outer walls of the grounds, and commanded by a window . . . the home of the resuscitated Avice." We may follow him on a subsequent evening when he is imagined walking down the lane to the *Red King's Castle* and searching for the names of Avice and Jocelyn, cut by himself years ago on one of the blocks of stone which had once formed a portion of the castle, but which now lay on the cliff-side below.

A further interval of time, during which our principal characters are in London and elsewhere, and we again visit Portland. Pierston is imagined to be staying for a time at *Budmouth*, and he frequently journeys to the Island. It is now that he becomes acquainted with the third Avice. *Henry the Eighth's Castle*, which we look on as the fictitious presentment of Sandsfoot Castle, comes before us again as the stage of events. Here, "on the verge of the ragstone cliff," Pierston meets Avice – at the same spot where he had arranged to meet the first Avice forty years previously. Hope Cove, the beautiful little bay which we have already regarded from Church-Hope, marks the spot from whence Avice and Leverre are supposed to have escaped in a rowing boat that had neither oars nor sails. It will be remembered that they came perilously near being drowned, for they had drifted very close to the Race, that dangerous current which even large vessels avoid in rough weather, and which is dangerous to small boats at any time. Its churned waters and white-capped waves may be seen most readily from the Beal, looking towards the Shambles, a sandbank lying towards the south-east.

It is at Portland that we first become acquainted with

Pierston, and here likewise we catch our last glimpse of him, living in a house at "the top of the Street of Wells" – a house we cannot identify with any certainty – and strolling with Marcia "towards the Beal, or the ancient Castle."

The Souls of the Slain

All in harmony with the weird, profound thoughts which fill this poem is the wild, forlorn aspect of Nature at Portland Bill, its background. To the solitary seer who muses here on the rocky headland comes the phantasma-gorical procession of "frameless souls," and we have but to visit the spot when the sombre shades of darkness are closing down upon it to picture ourselves that self-same crowd of hurrying spirits. We may then readily imagine them flitting in and out the dark caverns or hovering over the opalescent sheen which marks the Race – out there to the south-east, towards the Shambles. In summer-time, by daylight, the rocks take on a less forbidding aspect and the sea is in a calm mood. But in winter, and especially at dusk, when the waves are piling themselves on each other and angrily lashing the rocks, to fall back disappointed, yet, in fancy, not disheartened – then is the time to enter into our author's imaginary picture and comprehend somewhat of its significance.

THE
COUNTRY
OF
"DESPERATE REMEDIES"

The first landscape of any importance in this novel is before us when we hear of the characters at *Budmouth*, a place already mentioned as being more or less typical of Weymouth; and here we find the bay and the esplanade figuring as the principal backgrounds. If we follow Springrove and Owen and Cytherea Grey on the occasion when they take the excursion steamer to *Lulstead Cove*, we shall recognise a spot we have already visited when exploring the country of "Far from the Madding Crowd," this being the Cove where Troy bathed and was thought to have been drowned. We declared it then to symbolise Lulworth Cove. After they reach their destination we read that Owen goes off to visit "an interesting mediaeval ruin," and we have little doubt that our author refers to Corfe Castle. Finding it is too late to catch the return boat he walks on to *Anglebury* – a place we shall refer to later. Returning to the Cove, we watch the passengers re-embarking "by the primitive plan of a narrow plank on two wheels" – a method which may still be seen there to-day. Lulworth was once the scene of considerable smuggling operations, the residents in the few thatched cottages combining fishing and smuggling as their means of livelihood; but the little village is becoming rapidly crowded with week-end cottages and villas, which do not add to its picturesqueness or its charm.

Very soon after the *Lulstead* episode we see Springrove and Cytherea boating in *Budmouth Bay*, following the long line of ragged chalk cliffs which forms such a delightful background and accentuates the blue of the water. They pass *Creston* (doubtless Preston) beach and stop opposite *Ringsworth Shore* – suggestively Ringstead.

The action now moves inland and our interest is claimed by *Knapwater House*. This was probably suggested as Kingston Maurward House, which stands in a magnificently timbered park containing some fine specimens of lime and other deciduous trees. The house was built by a cousin of William Pitt at the end of the eighteenth century. When George III. was once paying a visit there, he is reported to have been asked by Pitt what he thought of the house, and to have replied: "Only brick, Pitt, only brick!" The result of this criticism was soon apparent, for Pitt had the whole house encased with a shell of stone, fixed to the

Kingston Maurwood House
(Knapwater House)
"The house was regularly and substantially built of clean grey freestone throughout, in that plainer fashion of Greek classicism which prevailed at the end of the last century." Just off the A35 at Stinsford is the *Knapwater House* of the novel. Today it houses the Dorset Farm Institute.

Kingston Park

brickwork with copper clamps. We read that "the house was regularly and substantailly built of clean grey free-stone throughout," a description we verify when we examine it.

If we can obtain permission to explore in Kingston Park we shall find much to interest us. The house, which has a stately, dignified appearance, stands on an eminence, the ground sloping away from it in all directions; a delightful lawn on the south side leads down to the lake, a fine sheet of water margined by timber trees and an undergrowth of rushes, reeds, and irises, beautiful indeed in spring when their masses of yellow flowers reflect the sunlight. On the water are mallards, coots, moorhens, and little grebes, sailing about among the herbage and disappearing mysteriously at the first indication of danger. If we turn eastward along the path that skirts the water, we shall soon see on our left hand a summer house – evidently the one which suggested "the Fane, built . . . in the form of a Grecian temple." (It is in fact called "The Temple" to this day.) Near it is the water-wheel (now closed in) giving out its continuous, monotonous throbbing. A little farther, and the path winds through thick undergrowth and emerges at the end of the lake, where the water empties itself in a cascade. From this spot we catch a glimpse of the old Manor-House – recently illustrated in an architectural work on Tudor mansions – which stands to us for the building where Manston lived; and as we walk towards it we are struck with a sound that is realistically suggestive of the duet which greeted Cytherea's ears on her arrival – a blended sound of the waterfall and the pumping engine.

The old building now before us has obviously seen better days. It belonged originally to the Grey family, from whom it passed with the estates to the Pitts by the marriage of George Pitt to Laura, only child and heiress of Audley Grey. The story tells us of the restoration of this Tudor building, which had fallen so low as to be "contained under three gables and a cross roof behind." It has passed through many changes since that time, but even to-day it exhibits a certain old grandeur which speaks to us of its past.

On the side of the lake remote from the house is a public footpath leading from Dorchester to Bockhampton, and from it we obtain an excellent view of *Knapwater House*, with the lake in the foreground, and the slope of greensward behind it in the middle distance. Perhaps it was on this path that Springrove was supposed to be standing when he wished Cytherea farewell and their hands met across the stream. There are many associations connected with this path, for it figures in the poem

THE
COUNTRY
OF

"THE HAND OF ETHELBERTA"

(A Comedy in Chapters)

The landscapes which form the environment in this lively book are to be discovered chiefly in Dorset, or South Wessex. The towns which figure have become fashionable seaside resorts since the date of the story, and consequently we must be prepared to find considerable alteration in the places described. The action commences at *Anglebury* – approximately Wareham – where we are introduced to that "old and well-appointed Inn," the "Red Lion," a building of imposing appearance standing at the crossroads in the centre of the town. This inn receives repeated mention and forms a convenient halting-place or half-way house between Swanage and Bournemouth. Wareham is a sleepy little town – in fact, it used to be said that the inhabitants only got up once a week, on market days! The town is almost surrounded by earthen walls; whether these are of Saxon or British construction is open to question, though it is generally supposed they are pre-Saxon. A local legend tells us that they were built to imprison the cuckoo, which was always supposed to arrive on Wareham Fair Day; and it is alleged that the townspeople, annoyed because the bird did not stay within the town limits, determined to construct earthen walls to shut it in. This was accordingly done, and the following year the bird duly arrived on the proper day, but soon flew away, just skimming over the top of the wall; whereupon one of the builders said: "Ther' now, if we'd a-builded they walls zix inches higher he 'ouldn' never have a-vleed away."

The town was occupied from very early times, and in 876 was held by the Danes. There was once a priory here, said to have been founded by St. Aldhelm, Bishop of Sherborne, about 701. There was also a castle prior to the Norman Conquest, the site being still visible. Wareham was accounted a borough in Domesday Book. The port was important in the Middle Ages, and during the French war in 1334 it was required to furnish four ships. Of the churches, that of St. Martin, exhibiting Saxon and four other styles of architecture, is the most interesting.

We read of Ethelberta starting from the inn for a country walk with, according to the hostler, "a clane-washed face,

The Red Lion, Wareham
(Anglebury)
The "old and well-appointed Inn"
is little changed, on the outside at
least: a "convenient halting-place
or half-way house between
Swanage and Bournemouth."
(Lea)

her hair in buckle." She pauses for a while on the bridge spanning the Froom, and then crosses the railway and follows the right-hand road. Presently she is distracted by the sight of a wild duck pursued by a hawk, and follows the birds across the heath until she comes close to "a whitely shining oval of still water, looking amid the swathy level of the heath like a hole through to a nether sky." We may recognise the spot in its likeness to Morden Decoy, some three miles from Wareham to the north-west. Here she meets with Julian, who was on his way to *Flytchett* – suggestively Lytchett Minster.

Sandbourne, which we have decided to regard as the counterfeit of Bournemouth, and the somewhat distant tract of water-meadow, marsh, and heathland – known in the book as *Sandbourne Moor*, and brought rather nearer to the town than in reality – forms the next background. In this town of mushroom growth we cannot hope to find the actual houses which served our author for models; the moor, too, has now been built upon to such an extent that its old-time characteristics are scarcely traceable.

"Three or four miles out of the town" and "over-looking a wide sheet of sea" stood *Wyndway House*. The description strongly suggests Upton House, and a good view of it can be had from the railway between Hamworthy and Poole stations. It is here that Julian and his sister are represented playing for the dancing. On their journey back to *Sandbourne* they catch a glimpse of Ethelberta and Picotee walking along the shore of a sandy nook, doubt-less on the harbour shore towards the Sandbanks, which the road would have overlooked.

Rookington Park is described as "abounding with timber older and finer than that of any spot in the neighbour-hood." From this we are inclined to place it as Hern Court, near Christchurch.

The house in which Ethelberta lived for a time with her mother and the children was the lodge of a newly-built house on the borders of the *Great Forest* – our author's pseudonym for the New Forest – known as *Arrowthorne Lodge*. It appears to be meant for one of the modern mansions in the neighbourhood of the wood called "The Earldoms," on the north side of the New Forest, between Romsey and Fordingbridge. There are, however, no distinctive features described by which we may recognise the individual mansion.

Such scenes as are supposed to take place in ordinary London houses we may ignore. Cripplegate Church is of course easily found, but the houses mentioned are too vague to be discoverable.

Farnfield is approximately Farnborough, where Neigh

Peter's Finger Inn, Lytchett Minster *(Flychett)*
That "trumpery small bit of a village".

The Mill Pond, Swanage
(Knollsea)
"A seaside village, lying snug within two headlands, as between a finger and thumb." Here were staged several scenes in Ethelberta's life. Though much has changed since the novel was set, the mill pond remains to be seen today.

had his "little place" and where Ethelberta in a moment of rash enthusiasm went to "spy out the land." The actual spot is naturally not to be found now, after years of building, but is quite typical of grounds when laid out before the mansion is erected.

The action again brings us back to South Wessex, with *Knollsea* as the background. This is virtually Swanage, once a mere fishing village, now a rising watering-place. The streets are sadly disfigured with newly erected buildings of a blatant style of architecture which utterly spoils the ancient picturesqueness of the place. Our author describes it as "a seaside village lying snug within two headlands as between a finger and thumb," a description which we find particularly apposite. The most interesting portion of the town nowadays centres at the old church, close to which is the mill, and several stone-built and stone-roofed cottages – all congruous with the date when Ethelberta is imagined to have visited the little town. We note with regret the widowerhood of "Old Harry," one of the several rocky pinnacles which jut out at the Foreland. They are formed of chalk and flints, and the sea is constantly eating out the foundations. "Old Harry's wife" – a companion rock – subsided from this cause, falling down one night during a terrific gale – well remembered in Swanage from the fact that the life-boat was wrecked the same night. These two rocky pillars are known in Studland, a village just round the Foreland, by opposite titles, the Studland folk maintaining it is Old Harry himself who has gone, his wife who remains. The differing opinions lead to interesting remarks from the two sets of thinkers! The clock-tower, which stands between the pier and coast-guard station, stood once on London Bridge; but a new and not too appropriate canopy takes the place of the original spire. The façade of the Town Hall was brought from Mercers' Hall and was designed by Wren. The cottage in which Ethelberta is supposed to have stayed with her brothers and sisters has been altered into a more modern structure, and now passes by the name of "Durlston Cottage."

Let us track Ethelberta when she goes on her memorable excursion to *Corvesgate Castle*, the counterfeit presentment of Corfe Castle. She starts along "a path by the shore . . . and thence up the steep crest of land opposite." We see her, after resting for a while, "turning to the left along the lofty ridge which ran inland, the country on each side lay beneath her like a map . . . through a huge cemetery of barrows, containing human dust from prehistoric times." We have little difficulty in recognising Nine-barrow Down, where tradition says nine kings or chieftains were

Corfe Castle (*Corvesgate Castle*)
"The towers of the notable ruin
rose out of the furthermost
shoulder of the upland, its site
being the slope and crest of a
smoothly nibbled mound at the
toe of the ridge."

The Way to Wareham

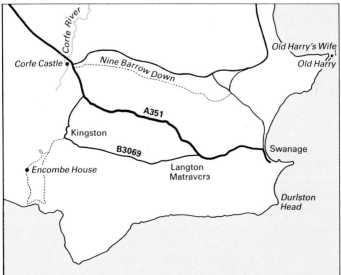

killed in one great battle against the Romans, and were buried, each in one of the nine barrows. We are told of the strange diversity of country which greeted Ethelberta's eyes on both sides of the ridge. The long high down seems to form a line of demarcation separating two very dissimilar types of landscape. On the northern side of the hill is a vast stretch of heath, and beyond it the serrated margin of Poole Harbour, with its islands, some treed, others bare, and in the distance the cliffs of Bournemouth. On the southern side we are greeted by the Purbeck Hills, and behind them the open sea. The different aspects are accentuated by the contrasts in lighting which the opposite sides of the hill obtain.

We will follow Ethelberta as she walks along the top of the ridge and descends into the village. In imagination we watch her as she "crossed the bridge over the moat and rode under the first archway into the outer ward . . . ascending the green incline and through another arch into the second ward." Then, after a further climb on foot, she is among the "windy corridors and mildewed dungeons," wherein Peter the Hermit, Edward II., and King John were once prisoners. The history of this ancient castle is too long to enter into now; it is scarcely necessary to say that after many vicissitudes it was blown up at the time of the Commonwealth, since when it has remained in ruins.

Enkworth Court by its ascribed position suggests Encombe; it was the seat of Lord Mountclere in the story, and the description of its site at least answers fairly well to that of Encombe House. But as to the building itself, the reader needs to be reminded of the remark, in my Introduction, that realities form only a peg for the depicted places to hang on, these latter existing nowhere outside the books. Thus the marvellous staircase said to be contained in the present building is either imported from elsewhere or is a pure figment of the author's imagination.

Melchester, representing Salisbury, figures so prominently in "Jude the Obscure" [see Volume 1] that we need now merely notice the "Red Lion" and the "White Hart," both well-known hostels bearing their legitimate names. It was in the Cathedral close that Ethelberta is supposed to tell Christopher of her intended marriage; and inside the Cathedral she is reconciled to Mountclere and promises to marry him on a definite date.

This leads up to a wild crisis in her life, and we read of her brothers, accompanied by the brother of Mountclere, trying to prevent the marriage. We may watch them, imaginatively, leaving London and arriving at *Sandbourne*, and we may follow them in their abortive attempt to reach *Knollsea* by steamer and their subsequent return to

St Martin's Church, Wareham
(Anglebury)
"Of the churches, that of St
Martin, exhibiting Saxon and four
other styles of architecture, is the
most interesting." (Lea)

Sandbourne. Thence they determine to post. First crossing *Sandbourne Moor* – where Picotee had so often met Julian earlier in the history – passing *Wyndway House*, leaving *Havenpool* – practically Poole – on their left hand, its "eyelets of light winking to them in the distance from under a nebulous brow of pale haze," they come to *Flychett*, that "trumpery small bit of a village" which we have held as being more or less akin to Lytchett Minster. Here they rest the horses at the inn called "Peter's Finger" – a house which still exhibits a swinging sign characteristic of its name, a corruption of *St. Peter ad Vincula*. In due course they reach *Anglebury*, where once again we see our old friend Hostler John coming from under the "shadowy archway" of the "Red Lion" and viewing the "mighty ekkypage" bowling towards him at that early, "purblinking" hour. With fresh horses they continue their harum-scarum journey to *Corvesgate Castle*, where they climb the steep ascent leading to *Little Enkworth* – perhaps Kingston Village – and pass on to *Enkworth Court*. Frustrated here, we see them hurrying towards *Knollsea* and reaching the church with its "square unembattled tower" too late to prevent the marriage.

The action goes back to *Enkworth Court*, and then to the "Castle Inn" at *Corvesgate Castle*. This inn, passing under the same name to-day, stands at the end of the street nearest to Swanage and still retains much of its old-time appearance. With Christopher we pay a last visit to *Enkworth Court* and catch a glimpse of Ethelberta – "her bonnet, her shoulders, her – but no more." Then going by steamer from *Knollsea* we pass "Old Harry" and reach *Sandbourne*. There are numbers of "Fir-top villas" at Bournemouth now, and it is useless to attempt to isolate the particular one from which the house in the story is drawn.

THE
COUNTRY
OF
"THE DYNASTS"

For obvious reasons there will be no attempt made in this Guide-book to conduct the reader over the Continental scenery which forms the bewildering variety of theatres for the huge Epic-Drama that lie outside England and its surrounding waters. The action of the drama in this country alone will take us over a wide stretch of land, and we shall revisit certain places which we have already examined in some of the previous novels and poems. The fresh features introduced demand our interest, and we shall look on them from new standpoints and in different lights.

The first scene of the first act of "The Dynasts" is not mentioned by any distinctive name, but its description enables us to recognise it as having been planned and drawn from the summit of Ridgeway Hill, midway between Dorchester and Weymouth. We have visited the spot when with our friends from *Overcombe* we climbed over the downs to see King George and his retinue pass by. This time we are drawn hither in order that we may overhear the converse of the stage-coach passengers in the pause at the top of the hill.

If at the present day we approach the hill from Dorchester we shall notice, just before the actual summit is reached, a track on the right-hand side. This was the old road, and it passed over the ridge and descended somewhat abruptly into the village of Upwey, where its junction with the newer road is readily seen. It is with the older track that we are concerned. It has not been mended for many years, and portions of it are now covered with grass. As we commence the descent a wonderful panorama lies before us. The Isle of Portland rises out of the sea, looking grim and forbidding, and between it and the Ridgeway the roofs of Weymouth glitter in the sunlight, while myriad sparkles are reflected from the bay and the lake-like inlet known as the Backwater. On our left hand lies Bincombe Down, its rounded barrows "like the bosoms of an amazon" standing clearly out against the skyline. To the right of Weymouth we catch glimpses of the Chesil Beach and the long sweeping curve which forms the shore-line of West Bay, or *Dead-man's Bay*. It is not until we descend lower, however, that other features,

Ridgeway Hill
The site of the opening scene of
The Dynasts.

now hidden by the Ridgeway itself, are uncovered.

The world ridge is here used in its purest meaning. Its course is marked by innumerable barrows, and a walk along the *rucke*, or back, from this point to the monument which tops Blackdown will repay us with a view not easily equalled in any part of Wessex.

It is while we listen in imagination to the discourse of the passengers that we learn of the proposed visit of the Court to "King George's Watering-place" (the periphrase used in this drama for Weymouth) – and thus the fact of there being "a deal of traffic over Ridgeway" is accounted for. At that date the minds of all who dwelt near the coast were perturbed with thoughts of Napoleon's arrival; and much speculation was rife regarding the actual spot at which the landing would be accomplished. This daily and hourly dread is vividly brought before us in "The Trumpet-Major," as well as in the poem entitled "The Alarm," already alluded to.

In the fourth scene of the second act we are on Bincombe Down hard by – the *Overcombe Down* of "The Trumpet-Major," and the same background as served for the short story entitled "The Melancholy Hussar of the German Legion." Our first impression on reaching the top of the hill is its changelessness. Here, among the barrows wherein our ancestors or their enemies lie sleeping, is a slice of the world which seems never to have been tampered with by human agency; we imagine it to have been thus through countless ages, and it is difficult to think of it as ever becoming other than it is to-day.

The name Bincombe is supposed to be derived from the English-Saxon word Binan-Comb, meaning the inside dell, and doubtless refers to the contour of the hill. In the description of the scene (using the word in its oldest and purest sense as denoting a platform) we read: "The down commands a wide view over the English Channel in front of it, including the popular Royal watering-place (Weymouth) with the Isle of Slingers (Portland) and its roadstead, where men-of-war and frigates are anchored," etc. If we will examine this description in the light of to-day we shall find it true to the letter; excepting that the old men-of-war and frigates are now represented by cruisers, Dreadnoughts, and torpedo boats.

This is where the review takes place; the king, now in residence at *Gloucester Lodge*, rides up on horseback to witness it, and his presence is viewed with consternation by some of his loyal subjects, who fear lest he should fall into Napoleon's clutches; for one of the spectators declares: "Gloucester Lodge could be surrounded, and George and Charlotte carried off before he could put on

**The Gloucester Hotel,
Weymouth** (Gloucester Lodge)
The building where the king
discussed "matters of cogent
state importance with Pitt".

his hat, she her red cloak and pattens!" The review – historically accurate – was a monster one of the first years of the nineteenth century; the line is said to have extended three miles. The plateau is sufficient to accommodate a vast concourse of people; its space is divided here and there by stone walls composed either of thin upright slabs or of rubble stone built with dry joints.

The down – so little altered in its general aspect – has seen many a military camp pitched and struck upon it since then; its surface has been scored by the hoofs of gaily caparisoned charges, as, earlier, by the foot of uncivilised man; but it probably never looked so gay or was so thickly populated as in the days when George III. was king, and when the dread Napoleon, "that arch-enemy of mankind," was daily expected to run his flat-bottomed boats on the beach that lay in view of its summit.

Standing here, more than 500 feet above the sea, with the aid of a glass we can make out a large number of spots in the surrounding country which figure in the Wessex Poems and Novels. The *Isle of Slingers* lies, "like a whale on the sea," due south of us; Hope Cove and the Beal and the Race are hidden from us, and only the Castletown heights, with the fort showing above, are conspicuous. Between us and the Island lies *Creston Shore*; almost at our feet is the little church of Bincombe, marking the resting-place of Phyllis Grove and Matthius Tina and his comrade. Sweeping westward with the sun, the narrow neck of pebbles that connects Portland with the mainland comes in, forming a portion of the Chesil Beach, and flanked on the east by Portland Roads, on the west by *Dead-man's Bay*.

Nearer to us is the "Royal Watering-place" of the drama, its blue bay rounding before it. Through our glasses we can distinguish the esplanade, *Gloucester Lodge*, the king's residence – now the Gloucester Hotel – and near it is the statue of the king. The Nothe protrudes into the bay, justifying its name.

Farther to the right we can get more glimpses of the Chesil Beach, which terminates at Abbotsbury – the *Abbotsea* of Wessex nomenclature – whose actual position is marked by St. Katharine's Chapel on the hill of the same name. *Pos'ham*, or Portisham, the home and birthplace of Captain Hardy, lies a trifle nearer to us. Then, looking up the Waddon Vale (the scene for the poem entitled "The Lacking Sense"), we see the grim outline of *Black'on* with the Hardy Monument topping it – from which spot uprose the beacon flames which come before us in the next scene. Only the height of Ridgeway prevents us from looking on

Stinsford Church *(Mellstock Church)*

Maidon; but we can distinguish the notched outline of *Eggar-Dun*, far in the distance, *Pummery* lies right over *Durnover Great Field*, and close to it *Casterbridge*, due north. Here and there we can trace a small section of Long Ash Lane, but especially where it rises to *Higher Crowstairs Down*, on its way to *Ivell*.

Still carrying our gaze in the same direction we light on *Mellstock* Church, and the great house in *Knapwater Park*. The western portion of *Egdon Heath* becomes conspicuous, with Rainbarrows standing out strongly, backed by the *Yalbury Woods*; while under this lie the Froom-watered meadows, amid which we can just discern the roofs of *Blooms-End* and the *Quiet Woman Inn*. Bulbarrow is in the distance beyond, and far away rises the hill-town of *Shaston*. Still farther round, and we come upon the village of *Stickleford*; then Clyffe Clump and Bere Hill, and behind that *Greenhill*, where the fair is held, and behind that again the hills that shut out *Shottsford-Forum*. Right over *Wellbridge* we see the pottery chimney which is close to *Anglebury*, with a wide stretch of *Egdon Heath* between us and it; behind *Anglebury* is *Havenpool*, its harbour glittering in the sunlight; and away in the far distance is the shimmering green haze that marks the *Great Forest*.

Due east of us are the undulating Chaldon Downs, and beyond them we can see Nine-Barrow Down, where it dips to *Corvesgate Castle*. Preston Hill hides *Oxwell Hall* from us, also the village of *Nether-Moynton*; but Holworth stands out boldly, and from it we can trace the position of *Lulstead Cove*.

The fifth scene of the second act takes us to Rainbarrows. This is the spot which formed such an oft-recurring background in "The Return of the Native," at the commencement of which story it was the site of a fire, just as it is now. On the top of the largest of these barrows – once a neolithic burial-place – many a fire has flamed up to celebrate various events, its first kindling having originated probably in a religious ceremony, or perhaps even in a sacrificial rite; and later to honour the dead who were buried under the tumulus. That particular fire called a bonfire, which was ostensibly supposed to commemorate Gunpowder Plot, was doubtless a survival from prehistoric times, inaugurated at a date long anterior to that of Guy Fawkes. Another, more recent, reason for the lighting of a fire on some high hill or building may be found in its use as a form of signalling over long distances, and many of our highest elevations bear evidence of having played this part in the history of the country, for the remains of old beacon-towers and huts may still be distinguished. We may recall that the news of the fall of Troy was signalled by

Rainbarrows
This ancient Egdon Heath burial
ground is also associated with
The Return of the Native and the
poems, "By the Barrows" and
"The Roman Road". Hardy wrote:
"Something in the feel of the
darkness and the personality of
the spot imparts a sense of
uninterrupted space around."

a fire, then called a courier-fire. The name beacon has passed sometimes to the hill itself; Dunkery Beacon (scene of "The Sacrilege"), the apex of Exmoor, and many others testify to this.

The "Rainbarrows" under notice, like many other ancient burial-mounds, have been opened by unskilful hands; the interiors have been flung about on all sides, leaving the centres as cup-shaped depressions. Close beside the barrows was an old Roman road, the altitude of the heathery ridgeway having doubtless been selected on account of the wide outlook which it commands. In our author's description of the spot we learn that a house of turves with a brick chimney stood on the sheltered side of the barrow during the wars with Napoleon, and evidence remaining is the foundation on which the brick chimney-shaft was reared. These bricks have been gradually distributed far and wide, and have been lost in the growth of heather and bracken which clothes the tumulus and the extensive waste around it; but by diligent search we may still find some here and there.

We are told of the wide vista which extends before the gaze of any one standing on the summit of Rainbarrow in the following passage: "Something in the feel of the darkness and the personality of the spot imparts a sense of uninterrupted space around, the view by day extending from the cliffs of the Isle of Wight eastward to Blackdon Hill by Deadman's Bay westward, and south across the valley of the Froom to the ridge that screens the channel." If we climb to the top of Rainbarrow to-day we can, in a clear atmosphere, distinguish each of these points, excepting only the cliffs of the Isle of Wight, which are shut out from us by a growth of trees on a more distant part of *Egdon Heath.* Just as on Bincombe Down, so here we can identify many of those places which we have already examined at close quarters; *Yalbury Wood* hides from us the hills which surround *Abbot's Cernel,* where the Cerne Giant is cut out on the grassy hill-side. To the eastward is *Kingsbere Hill* – the spot towards which one of the beacon-keepers was continually directing his gaze; and just behind it rises above the tree-tops the tower of Charborough – the *Welland Tower* of "Two on a Tower." The tumuli which top Bincombe Down are easily distinguished; and farther to the west we can trace the long straight white road leading up to the top of the Ridgeway, where we were standing in the first scene. Parts of *Casterbridge* are open to us, and to the eastward of the town we obtain a glimpse of the gables and chimneys of Max Gate – the residence of our author – the Max turnpike-road passing close beside it. Blackdon Hill and

**Captain Hardy's House,
Portesham** *(Pos'ham)*
Due west of Upwey lies the
Captain's house, visited in the
novel by Bob Loveday.

Hardy Monument are also in sight.

Both there and on *Kingsbere Hill* were stored ricks of dry fuel, ready to kindle when the signal was given, and we shall remember that the beacon-keepers were considerably agitated as to which spot they ought to watch for the signal. The advent of Mrs. Cantle on the barrow led to the recital of some of the superstitions current regarding Napoleon: "They say that he lives upon human flesh, and has rashers o' baby for breakfast – for all the world like the Cernel Giant in old ancient times!" Then as now the mystery concerning the Giant of Cerne was profound; in "The Lost Pyx" [Volume 1] we have touched on this matter The illuminating remark of Jem Purchess, "He's come!" is followed by the immediate kindling of the Rainbarrow beacon-fire, and this is still burning when morning dawns and discloses many of the dwellers on the coast hurrying inland – as in the traditional accounts.

Both the first scene of the fourth act and the seventh scene of the fifth act are staged at Weymouth. In the former we are introduced to "a room in the red brick Royal residence known as Gloucester Lodge". A footnote tells us "this weather-beaten old building though now an hotel is but a little altered." The description of the various features visible from the windows of the building is so comprehensive as to necessitate no elaboration on the part of the present writer. A certain window in the front of the house used to be pointed out as being the one from which the king was wont to gaze on the crowds that promenaded the esplanade or played their old-time games on the yellow sands below. Here, at his favourite summer resort, we find the king discussing matters of cogent state importance with Pitt, and in the course of their meeting the king refers to "Lord Nelson's captain – Hardy – whose old home stands in the peaceful vale hard by us here." We have already visited Captain Hardy in his home at Portisham when in imagination we journeyed there with Bob Loveday in the book entitled "The Trumpet-Major". We are further interested in "Nelson's Hardy" by reason of his consanguinity with our author, although the latter's immediate forebears were at that time resident a long distance from Portisham.

The second time that Weymouth comes before us as a background in the present book is when we overhear a conversation between some of the boatmen and the burghers in an ancient hostel near the harbour, called the *Old Rooms Inn*. This inn is still discoverable, close to the quay on the other side of the harbour-bridge, with its Elizabethan details at the back; but its front has been modernised to a large extent, and would probably be

Fordington Church (*Durnover church*)
See "the grey tower of Durnover church hard by", which was lit up by the flames of the bonfire that burned the effigy of Napoleon. Hardy also refers to the "still-used burial ground of an old Roman city, whose curious feature was this, its continuity as a place of sepulture."

HMS Victory
"She is the best sailer in the service, and she carries a hundred guns." The old relic of Trafalgar. "It is with feelings of solemnity," writes Lea, "that we tread the self-same deck on which Nelson and Hardy paced." Today, the renovated ship, also a subject of *The Trumpet Major*, continues to attract much interest among the public.

scarcely recognisable by its habitués of the early nineteenth century.

Our interest now centres in the scene on board the *Victory*, and it is with feelings of solemnity that we tread the self-same deck on which Nelson and Hardy paced. Lying at rest in Portsmouth Harbour, and anchored nearly midway between Portsea and Gosport, its old-world appearance is strongly intensified by contrast with the modern battleships which may be seen almost alongside the old relic of Trafalgar. Near it is moored the *Alberta* – the boat in which Queen Victoria crossed to the Island, and the last boat on which she set foot – while just inside it rides the Royal Yacht. Thus the *Victory* is surrounded by honourable companions that have taken part in many a history-making episode.

We might well wish that the famous ship had not been tampered with, that this memorial to one of England's greatest men had been preserved to us intact, and without being subjected to modern utilisations. Its employment as a training-ship, however, has necessitated many alterations, and we see a somewhat ruthless disregard for the old in order to make room for the modern.

In making our way from the Hard to the ship we may either select a boat at haphazard, or inquire for one Samuel Munt, a direct descendant of one of Nelson's crew. Samuel's grandfather served on board the *Victory*, and, provided the old man is in the humour for yarning, he will tell us stories and details handed down to him by his grandfather, tales which seem to bridge time and to take us back to the very days when the *Victory* was crowded with brave and eager men, who looked on their captain with a regard that almost amounted to reverence.

On board, we still seem to inhale the atmosphere surrounding Nelson and Hardy and their gallant men. On the main deck close to the skylight of Nelson's cabin, is the brass tablet marking the spot where he fell. There is Hardy's cabin, and within it the barge, presented by Queen Victoria, in which his body was conveyed from Greenwich to Whitehall on its way to St. Paul's for burial. Many interesting prints, maps, and paintings are to be seen in the cabins, including a picture of the death-scene executed from a drawing made on the voyage home; it is heavily framed in oak, which was once part of the ship. The floor of the lower deck is the original one; in the cockpit we are shown the table on which the wounded were laid out ready for the surgeons.

Here, we read in Act V. Part I. of the book before us, in this "low-beamed deck" were the wounded men, "some groaning, some silently dying, some dead." The cockpit is

Shockerwick House
Situated just across the boundary of Wiltshire in Somerset, about 4 miles from Bath, Shockerwick House is now owned by the Duke of Newcastle. Its picture gallery provides the background in the drama against which William Pitt the Younger meets Wiltshire.

Fordington Vicarage (*Durnover Vicarage*)
Now converted into apartments.

still lighted by dim lanterns, giving it a strange appearance of rehabilitation, and by the faint glimmer we see the pile of wreaths which are placed there annually on the 21st October by Nelson's descendants, marking the place where he lay and conversed with Hardy, and where his final words were spoken.

The action now turns to London, then to Weymouth once more, and, for a short scene, to Shockerwick House. We find this grand old house, surrounded by its picturesque scenery, about four miles from Bath. It was formerly the seat of the Wiltshire family, and the Picture Gallery forms the background against which Pitt and Wiltshire stand out in the sixth act of this Part.

Passing over all the intermediate Continental fields of action we come to that of *Durnover Green, Casterbridge*. We were close beside its original (Fordington Green) when we were exploring the country of "The Mayor of Casterbridge." It is still an open space, but its environs have been encroached on and altered since the date when the bonfire was lighted and the effigy of Napoleon hanged on a rough gallows and burned. We are told that a huge crowd had assembled from all parts to witness the pageant. One man had come from *Stourcastle* – approximately Sturminster Newton – a distance of more than twenty miles, while many familiar faces are brought before us as we gaze in imagination at the throng. The old vicarage, against the garden door of which the vicar is represented to be leaning, is the ivy-shrouded house now standing opposite the new vicarage. As the flames rise up they illumine "the grey tower of Durnover church hard by", and it requires little imagination to enable us to picture the scene, and even to think we hear the huzzas and shoutings of the excited crowd which is gathered round the fire. It may be mentioned that, according to the Oxford Dictionary, bonfire is probably a corruption of bonefire and originally signified a fire of bones. The burning of an effigy seems to be a relic of pagan sacrifices, when people were burnt alive in order to appease the wrath of the gods.

The entrance of the mail-coach, bearing the stirring news that Napoleon had been given up to public vengeance and that "anybody may take his life in any way, fair or foul," leads us to the end of the scene. The effigy is "blown to rags," for the flames have reached the powder; the crowd disperses; the band marches away playing "When War's Alarms" (an air of the date); and, to quote our author's words, "the fire goes out and darkness curtains the scene."

After the Club Dance

"Black'on frowns east on Maidon." *Black'on* is a local pronunciation of Blackdown, the heathery upland from which the Hardy Monument rears itself. A climb to the top of the Monument will reward us with a magnificent outlook: the Needles on one hand; the Devonshire coast on the other; and all the intervening country, exhibiting to the eye many of the backgrounds to the Wessex Novels and Poems. Around us in the distance and mid-distance are several eminences where beacon fires blazed at the time when the landing of Napoleon was expected, as in "The Dynasts"; we look down on Maidon Castle and can follow each ridge and ditch. Retracing our steps to Dorchester, we pass close beside that ancient earthwork, which, according to recent research, appears to have been the achievement of three distinct epochs of history. And if we turn our gaze back after another mile or two, and it happens to be near the setting hour of the sun, we shall then obtain a true impression of the fact that "Black'on frowns east on Maidon" still, just as it did in the days when *Maidon* was the *Dunium* of Ptolemy.

PLACE NAME INDEX

Page numbers in italics refer to
photographs; italicized words
refer to Hardy's names for places.